The Democratic Defeat a Resounding Failure
Terrorism

DEMOCRACY IN DANGER , THE FIGHT AGAINST TERRORISM

@COPYRIGHT

PRINTED 2025

AUTHOR DANIEL FARCAS

TABLE OF CONTENTS

INTRODUCTION: DEMOCRACY UNDER SIEGE

DEMOCRACY IN DANGER: THE URGENT NEED FOR ACTIVE DEFENSE

In the modern world, democracy faces one of its greatest existential threats: **its own hesitation to defend itself with the same intensity as its enemies**. Today, democratic nations are not only under attack by conventional military forces but also by **ideological warfare, disinformation campaigns, and terrorist organizations that exploit the very freedoms that democracy provides**. The idea that democracy will prevail simply by virtue of its moral superiority is a **fatal misconception**.

José Rodríguez Elizondo warns:

"A democracy that does not defend itself with the same intensity as its enemies will not survive them."

For decades, democracies have relied on **legal frameworks, diplomatic negotiations, and multilateral institutions** to ensure peace. However, their adversaries—**terrorist groups, authoritarian regimes, and radical movements**—do not abide by these same rules. Instead, they manipulate them to gain strategic advantages. The international system, originally designed to prevent conflict, has been **weaponized against democracies**, making them more vulnerable than ever.

José Rodríguez Elizondo's warning about the survival of democracies is a stark reminder of the challenges they face in today's world. In a time where authoritarian regimes and terrorist groups are on the rise, democracies must be vigilant in defending themselves against these threats. Elizondo's statement highlights the importance of democracies being proactive in protecting their values and institutions, rather than relying solely on traditional methods of diplomacy and negotiation.

One of the key points that Elizondo makes is that democracies must defend themselves with the same intensity as their enemies. This means being willing to take decisive action to protect their interests and values, even if it means going against the norms of the international community. In a world where authoritarian regimes and terrorist groups are willing to exploit legal frameworks and multilateral institutions to further their own agendas, democracies must be prepared to do whatever it takes to defend themselves.

One of the biggest challenges that democracies face in defending themselves is the weaponization of the international system against them. Authoritarian regimes and terrorist groups have become adept at using international organizations and diplomatic channels to undermine democracies and advance their own interests. This has put democracies at a disadvantage, as they are often bound by rules and norms that their adversaries are willing to ignore.

In order to survive in this hostile environment, democracies must be willing to adapt and evolve. They must be willing to take bold and decisive action to protect themselves, even if it means going against the traditional norms of diplomacy and negotiation. This may require democracies to be more assertive in their foreign policy, and to be willing to take risks in order to defend their values and institutions.

Ultimately, Elizondo's warning serves as a reminder that democracies cannot afford to be complacent in the face of growing threats. They must be willing to defend themselves with the same intensity as their enemies, and to be proactive in protecting their interests and values. Only by being vigilant and proactive can democracies hope to survive in an increasingly hostile world.

THE BATTLEFIELD HAS CHANGED: WARFARE IN THE AGE OF IDEOLOGY

Hernán López points out:

"The battle for democracy today is not just fought on the battlefield—it is fought in media narratives, political discourse, and international diplomacy."

While democracies focus on diplomacy, **their adversaries have mastered the art of ideological subversion**. Warfare today is no longer confined to the trenches or military campaigns—it is being waged in:

- **Global media outlets**, where narratives are shaped to demonize democratic nations while excusing the actions of authoritarian regimes.
- **Universities and educational institutions**, where historical revisionism fosters resentment and radical ideologies flourish under the guise of social justice.
- **International organizations**, which disproportionately condemn democracies like Israel while ignoring egregious human rights violations in dictatorial states.

By failing to recognize the **shifting nature of war**,

democracies are losing a battle they are barely fighting. Their enemies are not seeking compromise or mutual understanding—they seek **victory by exploiting the weaknesses of democratic systems**.

THE ROLE OF TERRORISM IN THE WAR AGAINST DEMOCRACY

Terrorism has become one of the **most effective tools against democratic societies**, not just because of its ability to cause destruction, but because of the **political and moral paralysis it induces**.

Ron Brummer explains:

"A temporary ceasefire without dismantling terrorist infrastructure is just an opportunity for rearmament."

The international community often pressures democracies to **negotiate with terrorist organizations**, treating them as legitimate political entities rather than violent extremists. This not only **emboldens terrorist groups** but also **demoralizes democratic societies**, as they see their governments conceding to those who openly seek their destruction.

use violence and fear to achieve their goals, and they have no qualms about targeting innocent civilians. They operate with a clear agenda of spreading chaos and instability, and they will use any opportunity to further their cause.

A temporary ceasefire without dismantling terrorist infrastructure is essentially giving these groups a chance to regroup, rearm, and plan their next attack. It allows them to replenish their weapons, recruit new members, and strengthen their networks. In essence, it is a temporary pause in the conflict that only serves to benefit the terrorists.

Ceasefire

The ceasefire that was established in 1949 between Israel and its neighboring Arab countries was meant to bring an end to the hostilities that had erupted during the Arab-Israeli War. However, instead of leading to a lasting peace, the ceasefire has become a tool used by terrorist organizations to pressure Israel and further their own agendas.

Since the establishment of the ceasefire, terrorist groups such as Hamas and Hezbollah have used the relative calm to build up their arsenals and launch attacks against Israel. These attacks have resulted in the loss of countless innocent lives and have created a constant state of fear and insecurity for the people of Israel.

The ceasefire has also been used as a propaganda tool by these terrorist organizations to portray themselves as freedom fighters and Israel as the aggressor. This has led to a skewed perception of the conflict in the international community, with many people failing to recognize the true nature of the threat that Israel faces from these terrorist groups.

Despite the pressure that the ceasefire has placed on Israel, the country has remained steadfast in its commitment to defending itself against terrorism. Through a combination of military action and diplomatic efforts, Israel has managed to thwart numerous terrorist attacks and prevent further loss of life.

However, the victory for terror that the ceasefire has allowed cannot be ignored. The constant threat of attacks has taken a toll on the people of Israel, who live in fear of the next terrorist strike. The international community must recognize the true nature of the threat that Israel faces and stand in solidarity with the country in its fight against terrorism.

In conclusion, the ceasefire that was established in 1949 has become a pressure point for Israel, allowing terrorist organizations to further their agendas and launch attacks against the country. Despite this, Israel has remained resolute in its commitment to defending itself against terrorism. The international community must support Israel in its fight against terrorism and work towards a lasting peace in the region.

Throughout its history, Israel has been involved in numerous ceasefires with various terrorist groups and neighboring countries. While these ceasefires are often seen as a temporary solution to ongoing conflicts, they are ultimately a victory for terror. This essay will explore some of the key ceasefires in Israel's history and analyze how they have ultimately benefited terrorist organizations.

One of the most well-known ceasefires in Israel's history is the 2014 ceasefire with Hamas, the militant group that controls the Gaza Strip. This ceasefire was brokered by Egypt and the United Nations after weeks of intense fighting that resulted in the deaths of hundreds of Palestinians and Israelis. While the ceasefire brought a temporary halt to the violence, it ultimately allowed Hamas to regroup and rearm, leading to further conflict in the years that followed.

Another significant ceasefire in Israel's history was the 2006 ceasefire with Hezbollah, the Lebanese militant group. This ceasefire was brokered by the United Nations after a month-long war that resulted in the deaths of over a thousand Lebanese and Israeli civilians. While the ceasefire brought a temporary halt to the fighting, it ultimately allowed Hezbollah to strengthen its position in Lebanon and continue its attacks on Israel in the years that followed.

In both of these cases, the ceasefires were ultimately a victory for terror. By allowing terrorist organizations to regroup and rearm, the ceasefires only served to prolong the conflicts and increase the suffering of civilians on both sides. While ceasefires may be necessary to bring about a temporary halt to violence, they are ultimately a flawed solution to the underlying issues that fuel terrorism.

Israel's history of ceasefires with terrorist organizations has been marked by temporary truces that ultimately benefit the terrorists. While ceasefires may bring about a brief period of calm, they do little to address the root causes of terrorism and often serve to strengthen the terrorists' position. As Israel continues to navigate its complex relationships with its neighbors, it is important to consider alternative solutions that address the underlying issues that fuel terrorism and promote lasting peace in the region.

History has shown us time and time again that negotiating with terrorists without demanding the dismantling of their infrastructure only leads to more violence and bloodshed. The Oslo Accords between Israel and the Palestinian Liberation Organization (PLO) in the 1990s, for example, did not lead to lasting peace because the PLO did not fulfill its obligations to disarm and dismantle its terrorist infrastructure.

Similarly, the US withdrawal from Afghanistan in 2021 and the subsequent Taliban takeover of the country have shown that giving terrorist groups breathing room only allows them to grow stronger and pose an even greater threat to global security.

It is crucial for democracies to stand firm against terrorism and not give in to the pressure to negotiate without demanding the dismantling of terrorist infrastructure. This means holding terrorist organizations accountable for their actions, cutting off their sources of funding and support, and actively working to dismantle their networks.

A temporary ceasefire can be a valuable tool in conflict resolution, but only if it is used as a stepping stone towards lasting peace and security. Without addressing the root causes of terrorism and dismantling the infrastructure that allows these groups to thrive, a ceasefire is just a temporary respite that ultimately benefits the terrorists.

In conclusion, a temporary ceasefire without dismantling terrorist infrastructure is not a solution to the problem of terrorism. It is merely an opportunity for rearmament and further violence. Democracies must stand firm against terrorism and work towards lasting peace by holding terrorist organizations accountable and dismantling their networks. Only then can we truly achieve security and stability in a world plagued by terrorism.

Terrorist organizations like **Hamas, Hezbollah, and ISIS** do not play by the same ethical standards as democratic nations. They:

- **Target civilians deliberately**, knowing that democratic societies value human life and will struggle with the ethical dilemma of responding forcefully.
- **Use democratic legal systems against themselves**, exploiting human rights laws to shield their operations.
- **Receive direct and indirect funding** from international organizations that claim to promote peace but, in reality, perpetuate conflict.

Israel has been at the forefront of this fight, demonstrating that **counterterrorism must be proactive, not reactive**. However, rather than learning from Israel's experience, many Western democracies **condemn its defensive actions**, setting a dangerous precedent where democracies are expected to tolerate terrorism rather than eradicate it.

ISRAEL: A BLUEPRINT FOR DEMOCRATIC RESILIENCE

Nayib Bukele states:

"The best thing that can happen to the Palestinian people is the disappearance of Hamas, a group that has only brought destruction and suffering."

Israel is the **only democracy in the Middle East**, and for decades, it has been forced to defend itself from both **military attacks and relentless global scrutiny**. While many Western nations have the **luxury of debating counterterrorism policies from a distance**, Israel faces **daily existential threats**. Its security policies, intelligence strategies, and **public relations battles** offer invaluable lessons to other democracies:

- **Border security is non-negotiable**: Israel has shown that strong borders and strict immigration policies are not acts of aggression but necessary measures for national security.
- **Preemptive military action works**: Israel's ability to detect and neutralize threats before they escalate has saved countless lives, yet it is often criticized by nations that lack firsthand experience with terrorism.
- **Information warfare must be fought aggressively**: Israel has been a prime target of global disinformation campaigns that seek to delegitimize its right to exist. Rather than ignoring these attacks, it actively counters them through diplomacy and digital media strategies.

Western democracies often fail to acknowledge that Israel's security policies **are not born out of aggression, but necessity**. The expectation that democracies should always "hold back" in the face of aggression is a **dangerous double standard** that will ultimately lead to their downfall.

Western democracies often fail to acknowledge that Israel's security policies are not born out of aggression, but out of necessity. The expectation that democracies should always "hold back" in the face of aggression is a dangerous double standard that will ultimately lead to their downfall. Einat Wilf, an Israeli politician and author, has argued that Western democracies need to understand the unique security challenges faced by Israel and recognize that sometimes tough measures are necessary to ensure the safety and security of its citizens.

Israel is a small country surrounded by hostile neighbors who have repeatedly threatened its existence. The country has faced numerous wars and terrorist attacks, and its citizens live under constant threat of violence. In this context, Israel's security policies are not driven by aggression, but by the need to protect its people from harm. The Israeli government has a responsibility to ensure the safety and security of its citizens, and sometimes this requires taking tough measures to defend against threats.

However, Western democracies often criticize Israel for its security policies, accusing the country of being too aggressive or heavy-handed in its approach. There is a perception that democracies should always "hold back" in the face of aggression, even when their own citizens are at risk. This double standard is dangerous and ultimately undermines the ability of democracies to protect their citizens.

Einat Wilf argues that Western democracies need to recognize the unique security challenges faced by Israel and support the country in its efforts to defend itself. Israel is not an aggressor, but a small country fighting for its survival in a hostile region. The expectation that Israel should always show restraint in the face of aggression is unrealistic and unfair.

In order to ensure the safety and security of their citizens, democracies must be willing to take tough measures when necessary. This may involve military action, security measures, or other forms of intervention to protect against threats. It is important for Western democracies to understand that sometimes tough decisions are necessary to ensure the safety and security of their citizens.

Western democracies need to acknowledge that Israel's

security policies are not born out of aggression, but out of necessity. The expectation that democracies should always "hold back" in the face of aggression is a dangerous double standard that will ultimately lead to their downfall. It is important for democracies to support each other in their efforts to protect their citizens and recognize that sometimes tough measures are necessary to ensure their safety and security.

THE FAILURE OF INTERNATIONAL ORGANIZATIONS

Former Chilean Presiddnt of Cámara de Diputados ", Prifesor Marco Antonio Núñez Lozano emphasizes:

"We must demand accountability from the UN and other institutions that selectively apply justice."

International organizations, once founded on the principles of **human rights and global stability**, have become **politicized instruments that disproportionately target democracies while shielding autocratic regimes**. The United Nations, the International Criminal Court (ICC), and the UN Human Rights Council (UNHRC) are among the worst offenders:

- The **UNHRC passes more resolutions against Israel than any other country**, ignoring human rights abuses

in China, Iran, North Korea, and Venezuela.
- The **ICC selectively prosecutes democratic leaders**, while dictators who commit genocide, mass executions, and ethnic cleansing operate with impunity.
- The **United Nations Relief and Works Agency (UNRWA)** claims to assist Palestinian refugees, yet its infrastructure is used to incite hatred and finance terrorism.

Democracies **must stop legitimizing these institutions** if they continue to apply **double standards that weaken the free world**.

THE NEED FOR A STRATEGIC SHIFT

Sharren Haskel states:

"Israel is not just defending itself—it is defending the values of the free world against those who seek to dismantle them."

To survive, democracies must **fundamentally rethink their approach to security, national identity, and ideological warfare**. This means:

1. **Recognizing that ideological battles are just as dangerous as military ones**: Radical ideologies seeking to dismantle democracy **must be countered with the same urgency as armed threats**.
2. **Refusing to negotiate with terrorist organizations**:

Diplomacy has its limits, and engaging with those who openly seek the destruction of democracy only **strengthens their position**.
3. **Holding international organizations accountable**: Nations that disproportionately attack democracies while ignoring real human rights abuses **should not receive funding or legitimacy from democratic states**.
4. **Strengthening internal resilience**: Universities, media outlets, and civil institutions should be protected from **ideological infiltration that seeks to erode democratic values from within**.
5. **Adopting Israel's proactive defense strategies**: Instead of criticizing Israel's counterterrorism measures, Western nations should **study and implement them**.

A DEMOCRACY THAT REFUSES TO DEFEND ITSELF WILL NOT SURVIVE

Golda Meir famously said:

"Peace will come when the Arabs love their children more than they hate us."

Democracies are being **challenged on all fronts**, and their failure to act decisively is being interpreted as weakness. Nations that **refuse to defend their principles, borders,** and institutions will not survive.** Israel has demonstrated that **security and democracy are not mutually exclusive**—they are **interdependent**.

As history has shown, **appeasement does not lead to peace—it leads to destruction**. Democracies that **fail to recognize their enemies and hesitate to act will be consumed by them**. The time for **decisive, unapologetic defense of democratic values is now**.

In the modern geopolitical landscape, democracies face not only external adversaries but internal ideological subversion.

Historical precedents have shown that hesitation in confronting radical threats leads to long-term instability and decline.

Protecting the principles of democracy requires a balance between openness and the willingness to defend national sovereignty.

Sergio Micco emphasizes, 'The greatest weakness of democracy is its hesitation to defend itself against those who seek its destruction under the guise of human rights.'

In the modern geopolitical landscape, democracies face not only external adversaries but internal ideological subversion.

Historical precedents have shown that hesitation in confronting radical threats leads to long-term instability and decline.

Protecting the principles of democracy requires a balance between openness and the willingness to defend national sovereignty.

Ricardo Brodsky explains, 'True democracy is not just about elections; it is about protecting institutions from ideological manipulation and extremism.'

In the modern geopolitical landscape, democracies face not only external adversaries but internal ideological subversion.

Historical precedents have shown that hesitation in confronting radical threats leads to long-term instability and decline.

Protecting the principles of democracy requires a balance between openness and the willingness to defend national sovereignty.

J.J. Brunner states, 'In times of crisis, democracies tend to surrender their principles to the loudest voices, whether from within or outside.'

In the modern geopolitical landscape, democracies face not only external adversaries but internal ideological subversion.

Historical precedents have shown that hesitation in

confronting radical threats leads to long-term instability and decline.

Protecting the principles of democracy requires a balance between openness and the willingness to defend national sovereignty.

Michael Ehrlich warns, 'A democracy that does not understand the nature of its enemies will not survive them.'

In the modern geopolitical landscape, democracies face not only external adversaries but internal ideological subversion.

Historical precedents have shown that hesitation in confronting radical threats leads to long-term instability and decline.

Protecting the principles of democracy requires a balance between openness and the willingness to defend national sovereignty.

Andrés Tassara notes, 'When education becomes a tool for indoctrination instead of critical thinking, democracy is at risk.'

Andrés Tassara's statement, "When education becomes a tool for indoctrination instead of critical thinking, democracy is at risk," holds a significant truth that resonates in today's world. Education is meant to be a tool for enlightenment, empowerment, and critical thinking. It is through education that individuals are able to develop their own opinions, question authority, and contribute to a democratic society. However, when education is used as a means of indoctrination, where students are taught what to think rather than how to think, the very foundation of democracy is threatened.

One example of education being used as a tool for indoctrination can be seen in the Palestinian education system. In many Palestinian schools, students are taught anti-Zionism and antisemitism from a young age. They are fed a narrative that demonizes Israel and Jews, perpetuating hatred and conflict rather than fostering understanding and peace. This indoctrination not only hinders critical thinking but also perpetuates a cycle of violence and division.

Furthermore, there are instances where education is used to deny historical atrocities, such as the Holocaust. Shoah deniers seek to rewrite history and spread misinformation, often targeting vulnerable populations, including students. By denying the Holocaust, these individuals are not only distorting the truth but also undermining the importance of critical thinking and historical accuracy in education.

In order to safeguard democracy, it is crucial that education promotes critical thinking rather than indoctrination. Students should be encouraged to question, analyze, and form their own opinions based on evidence and reason. By fostering a culture of critical thinking, education can empower individuals to become informed citizens who actively participate in democratic processes.

In conclusion, Andrés Tassara's assertion that "When education becomes a tool for indoctrination instead of critical thinking, democracy is at risk," highlights the importance of promoting independent thought and intellectual curiosity in education. By resisting indoctrination and embracing critical thinking, we can uphold the values of democracy and create a more informed and engaged society.

PART I: FOUNDATIONS AND VULNERABILITIES OF DEMOCRACY

1. What is Liberal Democracy?

2. The Vulnerability of Democracies

3. Terrorism Versus Democracy

PART II: THE INTERNAL DECAY OF DEMOCRACY

4. The Woke Movement and the Erosion of Democratic

Values

5. The Weaponization of Human Rights Against Democracies

6. The Role of the Media: Narrative Control and Public Opinion

7. The Collapse of Multilateral Institutions and the UN's Moral Failure

PART III: DEMOCRACY UNDER ATTACK

8. Radical Islamism: An Existential Threat to the West

9. The Left's Alliance with Islamist Extremists

10. How the West Funds Its Own Enemies

11. Israel as a Case Study for the Future of Democracies

PART IV: CASE STUDIES – HOW DEMOCRACIES FAIL

12. Europe's Submission to Radicalism

13. Latin America and Radical Islam: The Influence of Hezbollah

14. The United States: The Silent Infiltration of Islamist Networks

15. The International Criminal Court and UNRWA: Tools of Terrorism

PART V: SOLUTIONS – SAVING DEMOCRACY

16. Actions Required for the Survival of Democracies

17. The Imperative of Redefining Human Rights Standards

18. A Call to Action: The Moral and Strategic Challenges Ahead

THE FUTURE OF DEMOCRACY IN A WORLD AT WAR

In the modern geopolitical landscape, democracies face not only external adversaries but internal ideological subversion.

Historical precedents have shown that hesitation in confronting radical threats leads to long-term instability and decline.

Protecting the principles of democracy requires a balance between openness and the willingness to defend national sovereignty.

Profesor Sergio Micco emphasizes, 'The greatest weakness of democracy is its hesitation to defend itself against those who seek its destruction under the guise of human rights.'

In the modern geopolitical landscape, democracies face not only external adversaries but internal ideological subversion.

Historical precedents have shown that hesitation in confronting radical threats leads to long-term instability and decline.

Protecting the principles of democracy requires a balance between openness and the willingness to defend national sovereignty.

The former ambassador Ricardo Brodsky explains, 'True democracy is not just about elections; it is about protecting institutions from ideological manipulation and extremism.'

In the modern geopolitical landscape, democracies face not only external adversaries but internal ideological subversion.

Historical precedents have shown that hesitation in confronting radical threats leads to long-term instability and decline.

Protecting the principles of democracy requires a balance between openness and the willingness to defend national sovereignty.

J.J. Brunner states, 'In times of crisis, democracies tend to surrender their principles to the loudest voices, whether from within or outside.'

In the modern geopolitical landscape, democracies face not only external adversaries but internal ideological subversion.

Historical precedents have shown that hesitation in confronting radical threats leads to long-term instability and decline.

Protecting the principles of democracy requires a balance

between openness and the willingness to defend national sovereignty.

Michael Ehrlich warns, 'A democracy that does not understand the nature of its enemies will not survive them.'

In the modern geopolitical landscape, democracies face not only external adversaries but internal ideological subversion.

Historical precedents have shown that hesitation in confronting radical threats leads to long-term instability and decline.

Protecting the principles of democracy requires a balance between openness and the willingness to defend national sovereignty.

Andrés Tassara notes, 'When education becomes a tool for indoctrination instead of critical thinking, democracy is at risk.'

Democracy, the most advanced political system in modern history, is under siege from external and internal forces. On the one hand, radical groups exploit democratic freedoms to weaken societies from within. On the other hand, democracies hesitate to take decisive action, fearing accusations of authoritarianism. This book explores the fundamental
threats facing democracies today, from ideological

subversion to terrorist infiltration.

clear and concise.'

Professor Sergio Micco emphasizes the importance of recognizing the greatest weakness of democracy, which is its hesitation to defend itself against those who seek its destruction under the guise of human rights. This hesitation can be seen in the reluctance of some democracies to take decisive action against extremist groups that use democratic freedoms to undermine the very foundations of democracy.

One of the key challenges facing democracies today is the rise of extremist ideologies that seek to exploit the principles of democracy to advance their own anti-democratic agendas. These groups often use human rights rhetoric to justify their actions, claiming to be fighting for the rights of marginalized groups while in reality seeking to undermine the democratic institutions that protect those rights.

In the face of such threats, democracies must be willing to defend themselves against those who seek to exploit their openness and tolerance for their own destructive ends. This requires a clear understanding of the difference between genuine human rights advocacy and the manipulation of human rights language for nefarious purposes.

Former ambassador Ricardo Brodsky's assertion that true democracy is about protecting institutions from ideological manipulation and extremism is particularly relevant in this context. Democracies must be vigilant in safeguarding their institutions from those who seek to subvert them, whether through violent means or through the manipulation of democratic processes.

In times of crisis, democracies must resist the temptation to surrender their principles to the loudest voices, as J.J. Brunner warns. Instead, they must uphold the values of democracy and human rights while also taking decisive action to defend themselves against those who seek to undermine those values.

The greatest weakness of democracy is its hesitation to defend itself against those who seek its destruction under the guise of human rights. Democracies must be vigilant in protecting their institutions from ideological subversion and extremist threats, while also upholding the principles of democracy and human rights. Only by striking a balance between openness and defense can democracies ensure their long-term stability and resilience in the face of internal and external challenges.

PART I: FOUNDATIONS AND VULNERABILITIES OF DEMOCRACY

1. What is Liberal Democracy?

Liberal democracy is built on the rule of law, the separation of powers, and the protection of fundamental rights. However, these very principles are increasingly being exploited by adversaries who seek to dismantle democratic societies.

2. The Vulnerability of Democracies

Democracies thrive on openness and debate but are vulnerable to manipulation. Radical movements, foreign adversaries,
and ideological extremists exploit democratic institutions, making it difficult to implement effective security measures.

3. Terrorism Versus Democracy

Terrorism exploits democratic weaknesses, creating fear and division. Governments struggle to balance security and civil liberties while facing backlash from human rights organizations. Israel serves as a case study in democratic resilience.

PART II: THE INTERNAL DECAY OF DEMOCRACY

4. The Woke Movement and the Erosion of Democratic Values

The rise of identity politics and cancel culture has weakened national unity. The prioritization of ideological purity over rational discourse has created an environment where dissent is silenced, and radical ideologies flourish.

5. The Weaponization of Human Rights Against Democracies

International institutions, originally designed to uphold justice, are now being manipulated to protect terrorists while
punishing democratic nations. This distortion of human rights law undermines global stability.

6. The Role of the Media: Narrative Control and Public Opinion

The mainstream media has abandoned neutrality in favor of ideological advocacy. Biased reporting shapes public perception, turning democracies into villains while providing cover for extremist groups.

7. The Collapse of Multilateral Institutions and the UN's Moral Failure

The UN and its agencies, including the ICC and UNRWA, have failed to act impartially. Instead, they perpetuate conflicts, empower extremist narratives, and disproportionately target Israel while ignoring authoritarian regimes.

PART III: DEMOCRACY UNDER ATTACK

8. Radical Islamism: An Existential Threat to the West

Radical Islamist movements seek to undermine democracy through legal and cultural means. Unlike traditional Islam, these groups reject democratic principles in favor of Sharia law and authoritarian control.

9. The Left's Alliance with Islamist Extremists

Paradoxically, Western leftist movements have aligned with radical Islamists. This alliance is based on a shared opposition to Western values and national identity.

10. How the West Funds Its Own Enemies

Despite clear evidence of terrorist activities, Western democracies continue to fund regimes and organizations that
support extremism. Foreign aid is being weaponized against the very nations that provide it.

11. Israel as a Case Study for the Future of Democracies

Israel's struggle against terrorism is a cautionary tale for other democracies. Its security measures, policies, and counterterrorism efforts offer valuable lessons for nations facing similar threats.

INTRODUCTION: DEMOCRACY UNDER SIEGE

In the modern geopolitical landscape, democracies face not only external adversaries but internal ideological subversion.

Historical precedents have shown that hesitation in confronting radical threats leads to long-term instability and decline.

Protecting the principles of democracy requires a balance between openness and the willingness to defend national sovereignty.

Sergio Micco emphasizes, 'The greatest weakness of democracy is its hesitation to defend itself against those who seek its destruction under the guise of human rights.'

In the modern geopolitical landscape, democracies face not only external adversaries but internal ideological subversion.

Historical precedents have shown that hesitation in confronting radical threats leads to long-term instability and decline.

Protecting the principles of democracy requires a balance between openness and the willingness to defend national sovereignty.

Ricardo Brodsky explains, 'True democracy is not just about elections; it is about protecting institutions from ideological manipulation and extremism.'

In the modern geopolitical landscape, democracies face not

only external adversaries but internal ideological subversion.

Historical precedents have shown that hesitation in confronting radical threats leads to long-term instability and decline.

Protecting the principles of democracy requires a balance between openness and the willingness to defend national sovereignty.

J.J. Brunner states, 'In times of crisis, democracies tend to surrender their principles to the loudest voices, whether from within or outside.'

In the modern geopolitical landscape, democracies face not only external adversaries but internal ideological subversion.

Historical precedents have shown that hesitation in confronting radical threats leads to long-term instability and decline.

Protecting the principles of democracy requires a balance between openness and the willingness to defend national sovereignty.

Michael Ehrlich warns, 'A democracy that does not understand the nature of its enemies will not survive them.'

In the modern geopolitical landscape, democracies face not only external adversaries but internal ideological subversion.

Historical precedents have shown that hesitation in

confronting radical threats leads to long-term instability and decline.

Protecting the principles of democracy requires a balance between openness and the willingness to defend national sovereignty.

Andrés Tassara notes, 'When education becomes a tool for indoctrination instead of critical thinking, democracy is at risk.'

Democracies are facing one of the greatest crises of the modern era. For centuries, they have championed human rights, economic progress, and freedom. However, these same strengths are now being weaponized against them by ideological movements, terrorist organizations, and international bodies that fail to hold authoritarian regimes accountable.

This book will examine the **multidimensional threats** facing democracies today:
1. **External threats**, including radical Islamist terrorism and foreign adversarial influences like China, Iran, and Russia.
2. **Internal threats**, such as ideological extremism, media manipulation, and the erosion of national identity.
3. **The failure of international organizations**, including

the UN and ICC, which disproportionately target democratic states while ignoring human rights abuses in totalitarian regimes.

By analyzing **historical precedents, contemporary case studies, and policy failures**, this book aims to offer solutions
to preserve democratic governance before it is too late.

PART I: FOUNDATIONS AND VULNERABILITIES OF DEMOCRACY

1. What is Liberal Democracy?

Liberal democracy is based on **rule of law, civil liberties, and checks and balances**. Historically, its evolution has been shaped by:
- **The Magna Carta (1215)**, which established the principle that the monarchy was subject to the law.
- **The American and French Revolutions**, emphasizing individual freedoms and representative government.
- **Post-World War II democracy expansion**, where democratic institutions spread globally but now face resistance from authoritarian influences.

Yet, democracy is not self-sustaining. It requires **active

defense against ideological subversion**, which will be explored in this book.

2. The Vulnerability of Democracies

Democracies are uniquely vulnerable because their openness can be exploited. Key vulnerabilities include:
- **Legal constraints**, which make it difficult to preemptively counter extremist threats.
- **Freedom of speech**, which is manipulated to promote anti-democratic rhetoric under the guise of human rights.
- **Electoral manipulation**, where foreign actors use disinformation to influence democratic processes.

Case Studies:
1. **The Russian interference in U.S. elections (2016, 2020)**, highlighting cyber warfare's impact on democratic integrity.
2. **Europe's handling of Islamist extremism**, demonstrating how laws protecting free expression have allowed radical preachers to operate freely.

PART II: THE INTERNAL DECAY OF DEMOCRACY

4. The Woke Movement and the Erosion of Democratic Values

The **woke movement**, initially focused on social justice, has evolved into a rigid ideological framework that undermines democracy:
- **Identity politics** replaces meritocracy, causing divisions rather than unity.
- **Cancel culture** silences dissent, preventing open discourse.
- **Institutional infiltration** erodes academic freedom and neutral journalism.

Historical Parallels:
- The **Cultural Revolution in China (1966-1976)**, where ideological purity led to mass censorship and societal division.
- The **Soviet Union's control of academia**, demonstrating how ideology-driven policies undermine national progress.

5. The Weaponization of Human Rights Against Democracies

International bodies such as the **UNHRC and ICC** have been co-opted by political interests. Instead of holding **actual human rights violators accountable**, they target democratic nations disproportionately.

Case Study:

- **Israel and the ICC**: While the ICC investigates Israeli military actions, it ignores systematic human rights violations in Iran and Syria.

Policy Recommendations:
1. **Require transparency in international organizations** to prevent biased resolutions.
2. **Create alternative international alliances** focused on genuine human rights advocacy.

1. WHAT IS LIBERAL DEMOCRACY?

Liberal democracy is the most advanced form of governance, yet its survival is not guaranteed. This chapter explores:
- **Origins of liberal democracy** – From the **Magna Carta (1215)** to the **Enlightenment thinkers (Locke, Montesquieu, Rousseau)**.
- **Principles of democracy** – The **rule of law, separation of powers, protection of rights**.
- **Challenges in the 21st century** – Globalization, digital disinformation, and ideological extremism.

2. THE VULNERABILITY OF DEMOCRACIES

Modern democracies face existential threats, both **external (terrorism, cyber warfare, foreign influence)** and **internal (identity politics, media bias, radicalization).**

Key Areas of Vulnerability:
- **Legal constraints** – How democratic laws prevent preemptive action against threats.
- **Freedom of speech vs. Hate speech** – When democracies struggle to define harmful ideologies.
- **Electoral interference** – Case studies on Russian, Iranian, and Chinese meddling in democratic elections.

3. TERRORISM VERSUS DEMOCRACY

Terrorist organizations **exploit democratic values** to advance their goals. They take advantage of **legal protections, human rights rhetoric, and open societies** to operate freely.

Key Topics:
- **The rise of radical Islamism in democratic societies** – Examples from **France, Belgium, the UK, and Germany**.
- **State-sponsored terrorism** – How **Iran, Russia, and North Korea** manipulate democratic weaknesses.
- **Israel as a case study** – The only democracy in the Middle East constantly under attack.

4. THE WOKE MOVEMENT AND THE EROSION OF DEMOCRATIC VALUES

Once rooted in social justice, the **woke movement has evolved into an authoritarian ideology** that threatens **free speech, meritocracy, and national cohesion**.

Analysis:
- **The shift from civil rights to radical activism** – How modern movements reject dialogue in favor of cancel culture.
- **Corporate and academic capture** – How major institutions have been pressured into ideological conformity.
- **Historical comparisons** – The parallels between woke ideology and **Mao's Cultural Revolution (1966-76)**.

5. THE WEAPONIZATION OF HUMAN RIGHTS AGAINST DEMOCRACIES

International institutions, including the UN and ICC, have been manipulated to target democracies while ignoring authoritarian regimes.

Key Cases:
- **Israel at the ICC** – Why the court focuses disproportionately on a democracy while ignoring war crimes in Syria, China, and Iran.
- **The hypocrisy of the UNHRC** – How nations like Venezuela, Iran, and North Korea sit on human rights councils.
- **Solutions** – Reforming international organizations to prevent anti-democratic manipulation.

6. THE ROLE OF THE MEDIA: NARRATIVE CONTROL AND PUBLIC OPINION

The media has become a **powerful political weapon**, often shaping narratives that weaken democracies.

Key Topics:
- **Media bias and selective outrage** – How coverage of the Israeli-Palestinian conflict exposes journalistic double standards.
- **Censorship and tech monopolies** – How social media platforms silence dissenting voices.
- **Propaganda in the digital age** – How extremist groups manipulate democratic media to promote their agenda.

7. THE COLLAPSE OF MULTILATERAL INSTITUTIONS AND THE UN'S MORAL FAILURE

The UN, ICC, and EU have failed to uphold democratic values and instead shield terrorist organizations.

Key Issues:
- **UNRWA and Hamas ties** – Evidence that UNRWA employs terrorist affiliates.
- **The ICC's failure** – Why the court ignores **Russia's war crimes** but aggressively prosecutes **Israel**.

- **Reforming global governance** – What democracies must do to restore fairness.

8. RADICAL ISLAMISM: AN EXISTENTIAL THREAT TO THE WEST

Islamist extremists **use democracy to destroy democracy**.

Key Topics:
- **How Sharia law conflicts with democratic governance**.
- **The Muslim Brotherhood's role in radicalizing Western communities**.
- **Terrorist recruitment strategies** – The role of **social media, mosques, and NGOs**.

9. THE LEFT'S ALLIANCE WITH ISLAMIST EXTREMISTS

The paradox of leftist-Islamist cooperation:
- **Common enemy: Western civilization** – Why the radical

left and Islamists share a desire to dismantle democratic structures.
- **Case studies:** The **Women's March, Black Lives Matter, and Democratic Socialists of America** embracing **anti-Israel rhetoric**.
- **Consequences for global stability** – How this alliance strengthens **authoritarian regimes**.

10. HOW THE WEST FUNDS ITS OWN ENEMIES

Western governments **unknowingly finance extremism** through aid programs, political appeasement, and weak immigration policies.

Key Cases:
- **Qatar and Turkey funding Islamist groups in Europe**.
- **The Palestinian Authority's 'Martyrs Fund'** – How Western aid money pays for terrorist salaries.
- **The failure of deradicalization programs** – Why soft policies have emboldened radicals.

11. ISRAEL AS A CASE STUDY FOR THE FUTURE OF DEMOCRACIES

Israel **faces unique challenges as the only democracy in the Middle East**, yet its **counterterrorism strategies offer lessons for the West**.

Topics:
- **Border security policies that work** – How Israel prevents terrorist infiltration.
- **Military strategy vs. political constraints** – The dilemma democracies face when fighting asymmetric warfare.
- **Public perception battles** – How Israel's media strategy counters misinformation.

Israel while ignoring the crimes of authoritarian regimes. This bias weakens democratic alliances and emboldens their adversaries.

In the face of these challenges, Israel serves as a critical case study for the future of democracies worldwide. Its experience illustrates the necessity of a robust defense against both external threats and internal subversion. As democracies grapple with the complexities of modern governance, they must learn from Israel's strategies in border security, military engagement, and public relations.

Border Security Policies That Work

Israel's border security policies are often cited as exemplary in preventing terrorist infiltration. The country employs a multi-layered approach that includes physical barriers, advanced surveillance technology, and intelligence operations. These measures have significantly reduced the number of successful attacks on its territory.

The lessons from Israel's border security can be applied to other democracies facing similar threats. Effective border control is not merely about physical barriers; it also involves comprehensive intelligence-sharing and cooperation with neighboring states. Democracies must recognize that a secure border is foundational to national sovereignty and public safety.

Military Strategy vs. Political Constraints

The dilemma of military strategy versus political constraints is a common challenge for democracies engaged in asymmetric warfare. Israel's military, the IDF, operates under strict ethical guidelines, balancing the need for security with the imperative to minimize civilian casualties. This ethical framework is crucial for maintaining public support and international legitimacy.

However, the political landscape often complicates military decisions. Leaders must navigate public opinion, international pressure, and the potential for backlash against military actions. Democracies must learn to balance these competing interests while remaining resolute in their defense against terrorism.

Public Perception Battles

Public perception plays a vital role in the ongoing conflict between democracies and extremist ideologies. Israel has developed a sophisticated media strategy to counter misinformation and promote its narrative on the global stage. This involves proactive communication, engaging with international audiences, and leveraging social media platforms to disseminate accurate information.

Democracies must recognize the importance of narrative

control in the information age. They must invest in public diplomacy and counter-narratives to combat radical ideologies that seek to undermine democratic values.

The only democracy In the midle east

As the only democracy in the Middle East, Israel's experiences offer invaluable lessons for democracies worldwide. The challenges it faces—ranging from border security to military engagement and public perception—are not unique but rather reflective of broader trends in global governance.

Democracies must learn to defend themselves vigorously while upholding their foundational principles. The battle for democracy is not just fought on the battlefield; it is fought in the hearts and minds of citizens, in the narratives that shape public discourse, and in the institutions that uphold democratic values.

In light of these insights, it becomes abundantly clear that the survival of democracy hinges not only on the ability to conduct free and fair elections but also on the resilience of its institutions against ideological subversion and external threats. The challenges faced by democracies today are multifaceted and complex, requiring a nuanced understanding of both the internal and external forces that seek to undermine them.

Sergio Micco aptly highlights a critical vulnerability within democratic systems: the tendency to hesitate in the face of aggression, often masked as a concern for human rights. This hesitation can lead to a paralysis that allows adversaries to exploit democratic values for their own ends. Democracies must recognize that defending their core principles does not equate to abandoning human rights; rather, it involves a robust commitment to safeguarding those rights against those who would undermine them. This delicate balance is essential for maintaining the integrity of democratic societies, especially in an era where the lines between legitimate dissent and subversive action can become blurred.

The historical context of democracy reveals that it is often under siege from those who would manipulate its principles for their own gain. This manipulation can take many forms, from radical ideologies that seek to delegitimize the very concept of democracy to authoritarian regimes that exploit democratic norms to gain power. The challenge for democracies is to remain steadfast in their commitment to their foundational values while also being vigilant against those who would seek to exploit these values for destructive purposes.

Ricardo Brodsky emphasizes that true democracy extends beyond the electoral process. It encompasses the protection of institutions that uphold democratic values. This protection is essential in an era where ideological manipulation can distort public discourse and erode trust in democratic processes. Democracies must be vigilant in defending their institutions from extremist ideologies that seek to delegitimize dissent and manipulate public opinion. The erosion of institutional integrity can lead to a slippery slope where the very foundations of democracy are compromised, making it imperative for citizens and leaders alike to actively engage in safeguarding these institutions.

The Israeli experience serves as a poignant case study in this regard. As the only democracy in the Middle East, Israel has faced relentless challenges from various extremist groups that seek to undermine its existence. The country's approach to counterterrorism, which includes a combination of military action, intelligence operations, and public diplomacy, illustrates the necessity of a multifaceted strategy in defending democratic values. Israel's military, the IDF, operates under strict ethical guidelines, balancing the need for security with the imperative to minimize civilian casualties. This ethical framework is crucial for maintaining public support and international legitimacy, yet it is constantly tested by the realities of asymmetric warfare.

In confronting these challenges, Israel has developed a sophisticated media strategy to counter misinformation and promote its narrative on the global stage. This involves proactive communication, engaging with international audiences, and leveraging social media platforms to disseminate accurate information. The importance of narrative control in the information age cannot be overstated; democracies must invest in public diplomacy and counter-narratives to combat radical ideologies that seek to undermine democratic values. The battle for public perception is as critical as any military engagement, as the narratives that dominate public discourse can shape policy decisions and influence international relations.

Moreover, the ideological battle extends beyond military engagements and media narratives. It is fought in classrooms, universities, and cultural institutions, where radical narratives can take root and flourish. As **Guillermo Holzman** points out, the global battle today is not just military; it is ideological. Democracies must recognize that failing to counteract these forces leaves them defenseless, not just against terrorism, but against internal decay. Education plays a pivotal role in this struggle; it must foster critical thinking and resilience against indoctrination. When education becomes a tool for ideological manipulation, democracies risk producing generations that are ill-equipped to defend their own values.

Senador Jaime Quintana warns that if democracies do not wake up to the double standards of international organizations, they will find themselves isolated in their own defense. The international community often applies human rights standards selectively, disproportionately targeting democratic states like Israel while ignoring the crimes of authoritarian regimes. This bias weakens democratic alliances and emboldens adversaries who seek to exploit these discrepancies. Democracies must unite in their defense of each other, recognizing that the struggle for one is the struggle for all. Solidarity among democracies is essential, as it reinforces the notion that the defense of democratic values is a collective responsibility.

Furthermore, ** the remarkable Chilean parliament, Diputado Miguel Angel Calisto** articulates a crucial point: the survival of democracy depends on its ability to distinguish between legitimate criticism and attempts to dismantle it. While self-criticism is a strength of democratic societies, it becomes dangerous when exploited by ideological actors who seek to delegitimize democratic institutions. Failing to recognize the difference between constructive debate and subversive propaganda leaves democracies vulnerable to their own openness. This is particularly relevant in an age where social media amplifies dissenting voices, often blurring the lines between genuine critique and harmful disinformation. The challenge lies in fostering an environment where constructive criticism can thrive without allowing it to devolve into a tool for subversion.

As **the layer and former parliament member Gabriel Silber** emphasizes, "A nation that abandons its historical identity will eventually abandon its moral compass." Democracies that fail to uphold their founding principles become vulnerable to ideological subversion. Without a strong historical identity, citizens lose sight of what they are fighting to protect, making it easier for radical movements to redefine national values in ways that weaken democratic institutions. This underscores the importance of fostering a collective memory and understanding of a nation's values and history, ensuring that citizens are equipped to defend them. A shared historical narrative can serve as a unifying force, reinforcing the commitment to democratic principles and the values that underpin them.

The role of civil society in this context cannot be overstated. A vibrant civil society is essential for the health of democracy, as it provides a platform for diverse voices and perspectives. Civil society organizations can play a crucial role in educating citizens about their rights and responsibilities, fostering civic engagement, and promoting a culture of accountability. By empowering citizens to actively participate in the democratic process, civil society can help to counteract the forces of extremism and ideological manipulation. This engagement is vital for ensuring that democracy remains responsive to the needs and concerns of its citizens.

In addition, the media plays a pivotal role in shaping public discourse and influencing perceptions of democracy. A free and independent press is essential for holding power accountable and providing citizens with the information they need to make informed decisions. However, the media landscape is increasingly fragmented, with the rise of social media creating echo chambers that can amplify misinformation and extremist narratives. Democracies must invest in media literacy programs to equip citizens with the skills to critically evaluate information sources and discern fact from fiction. This investment in media literacy is not just a safeguard against misinformation; it is a fundamental component of a well-functioning democracy.

As democracies navigate these challenges, they must also be mindful of the global context in which they operate. The rise of authoritarianism and populism in various parts of the world poses a significant threat to democratic values. Democracies must stand in solidarity with one another, recognizing that the fight for democracy is a global struggle. This solidarity can take many forms, from diplomatic support to economic partnerships, but it must be rooted in a shared commitment to uphold democratic principles and human rights.

In conclusion, as the profesor Michael Ehrlich warns, understanding the nature of enemies is paramount for the survival of democracy. Democracies must not only defend their values but also actively engage in the ideological battles that shape their future. By doing so, they can uphold their principles while effectively countering those who seek to dismantle them, ensuring a vibrant and enduring democratic society. The lessons drawn from Israel's experiences serve as a clarion call for democracies worldwide: to remain vigilant, to engage proactively in the ideological arena, and to fortify their institutions against both external threats and internal decay.

The fight for democracy is not merely a political struggle; it is a comprehensive endeavor that encompasses security, education, public discourse, and the unwavering commitment to uphold the values that define a free society. Democracies must cultivate a culture of resilience, where citizens are not only aware of the threats they face but are also equipped with the tools to confront them. This involves fostering a robust civil society that encourages active participation, critical thinking, and open dialogue.

Ultimately, the future of democracy rests on the ability of its citizens to recognize the fragility of their freedoms and the necessity of defending them. As history has shown, complacency can lead to vulnerability, and the failure to act decisively in the face of threats can result in the erosion of democratic values. By learning from the experiences of Israel and other democracies facing similar challenges, nations can forge a path forward that not only protects their current freedoms but also strengthens the foundations upon which those freedoms are built. The commitment to democracy must be unwavering, and the resolve to defend it must be as strong as the ideals it represents. Only then can democracies hope to thrive in an increasingly complex and hostile world.

In this context, it is also crucial for democracies to engage in continuous self-reflection and reform. The ability to adapt to changing circumstances and to address the legitimate grievances of citizens is essential for maintaining public trust and support. Democracies must be willing to confront their shortcomings and to make necessary adjustments to their systems and processes. This commitment to self-improvement is not a sign of weakness; rather, it is a testament to the strength and resilience of democratic governance.

Israel's experience with resilience in the face of security challenges, particularly regarding terrorism and conflict, provides several notable examples. These instances illustrate how the country has adapted and responded to threats while maintaining its societal cohesion and democratic values. Here are some key examples of resilience in Israel:

1. **Civil Defense and Emergency Preparedness**

- **Home Front Command**: Israel has developed a robust civil defense system, including the Home Front Command, which prepares citizens for emergencies such as rocket attacks and natural disasters. Regular drills, public education campaigns, and the establishment of bomb shelters have equipped the population to respond effectively to threats.

- **Public Awareness Campaigns**: The government conducts ongoing public awareness campaigns to educate citizens about emergency procedures, including how to respond during air raid sirens and the importance of having emergency kits.

2. **Technological Innovation**

- **Iron Dome**: The Iron Dome missile defense system is a prime example of Israel's technological resilience. It intercepts and destroys short-range threats, such as rockets fired from Gaza, thereby protecting civilian populations and reducing casualties. This system has been crucial in maintaining public safety during conflicts.

- **Cybersecurity**: Israel is a global leader in cybersecurity, with a thriving tech industry focused on developing solutions to protect against cyber threats. The country's emphasis on innovation and technology has helped it defend against various forms of attacks, including those targeting critical infrastructure.

3. **Community Cohesion and Support Systems**

- **National Solidarity**: During times of conflict, Israelis often demonstrate a strong sense of national solidarity. Community support systems, such as volunteer organizations and local initiatives, mobilize to assist those affected by violence, providing psychological support, food, and shelter.

- **Resilience in Daily Life**: Despite the ongoing security threats, many Israelis continue their daily lives with a sense of normalcy. Schools, businesses, and cultural activities often proceed as planned, reflecting a collective determination to maintain a vibrant society despite external pressures.

4. **Education and Awareness**

- **Civic Education**: Israeli schools incorporate lessons on resilience, national security, and the importance of democratic values. This education fosters a sense of responsibility among youth and prepares them to engage with complex societal issues.

- **Counter-Radicalization Programs**: Various initiatives aim to counter extremist ideologies and promote tolerance and coexistence among different communities within Israel. These programs often involve dialogue between Jewish and Arab youth, fostering understanding and reducing tensions.

5. **International Cooperation and Diplomacy**

- **Global Partnerships**: Israel has established strong security partnerships with various countries, sharing intelligence and best practices in counter-terrorism. This international cooperation enhances Israel's resilience by providing additional resources and support in addressing security challenges.

- **Peace Agreements**: Efforts to achieve peace agreements with neighboring countries, such as the Abraham Accords, demonstrate Israel's resilience in pursuing diplomatic solutions to long-standing conflicts. These agreements have opened new avenues for cooperation and stability in the region.

6. **Psychological Resilience**

- **Mental Health Services**: Recognizing the psychological impact of living under threat, Israel has developed mental health services to support individuals affected by trauma, including those who have experienced rocket attacks or terrorist incidents. Programs aimed at children and families help build resilience and coping mechanisms.

- **Cultural Resilience**: The arts, music, and cultural expressions in Israel often reflect themes of resilience and hope. Cultural events and festivals serve as platforms for unity and healing, reinforcing a collective identity despite challenges.

Conclusion

Israel's resilience in the face of ongoing security threats is characterized by a combination of technological innovation, community cohesion, education, and international cooperation. By fostering a culture of preparedness and adaptability, Israel has managed to maintain its democratic values and societal stability despite the challenges posed by terrorism and conflict. These examples of resilience can serve as valuable lessons for other nations facing similar threats, highlighting the importance of a multifaceted approach to security and community well-being.

Moreover, the role of education in shaping the future of democracy cannot be overstated. An informed and educated citizenry is the bedrock of a healthy democracy. Educational institutions must prioritize the teaching of democratic values, critical thinking, and civic responsibility. By instilling these principles in future generations, democracies can ensure that their citizens are equipped to engage thoughtfully and constructively in the democratic process. This investment in education is not just an investment in the future; it is a safeguard against the forces of extremism and authoritarianism that threaten to undermine democratic societies.

As democracies face the challenges of the 21st century, they must also recognize the importance of inclusivity and representation. A democracy that fails to represent the diverse voices and perspectives of its citizens is at risk of alienating significant segments of its population. This alienation can lead to disillusionment and disengagement, creating fertile ground for extremist ideologies to take root. Democracies must strive to create inclusive political systems that empower all citizens to participate in the democratic process, ensuring that their voices are heard and their concerns are addressed.

In summary, the future of democracy depends on a multifaceted approach that encompasses vigilance, education, inclusivity, and a commitment to self-improvement. Democracies must learn from the experiences of others, including Israel, and adapt their strategies to meet the challenges of an increasingly complex and hostile world. By doing so, they can not only defend their values but also promote a vision of democracy that is resilient, inclusive, and responsive to the needs of all citizens. The fight for democracy is ongoing, and it requires the active participation of all members of society. Only through collective action and a shared commitment to democratic principles can we hope to build a future where democracy not only survives but thrives.

The quotes from professor J.J. Brunner, professor Michael Ehrlich, Andrés Tassara, and Gabriel Zaliasnik encapsulate some of the most pressing challenges faced by democracies in the 21st century, particularly in the context of the so-called "woke generation." This term often refers to a heightened awareness of social injustices and a commitment to addressing systemic inequalities. However, it also brings with it a set of challenges that can complicate the landscape of democratic discourse and engagement.

J.J. Brunner's observation about democracies surrendering their principles in times of crisis speaks to a recurring theme in history: the tendency for democratic societies to prioritize immediate security or stability over their foundational values. This phenomenon can lead to the erosion of civil liberties, the curtailment of dissent, and the rise of authoritarian tendencies. When faced with crises—be they economic, social, or security-related—democracies may find themselves capitulating to the loudest voices, which often represent extreme or populist views. In the context of the woke generation, this can manifest as a demand for rapid social change that sometimes overlooks the complexities of democratic deliberation and the need for consensus-building. The urgency to address social injustices can lead to a polarization of opinions, where those who do not fully align with the prevailing narrative may feel marginalized or silenced.

Michael Ehrlich emphasizes the importance of understanding the nature of one's enemies. In an era marked by disinformation, radical ideologies, and geopolitical tensions, democracies must be astute in recognizing the threats they face. Failing to grasp the motivations and strategies of adversaries can lead to misguided policies and an inability to effectively defend democratic values. The woke generation, while often advocating for necessary social reforms, can sometimes inadvertently contribute to polarization by framing debates in binary terms—us versus them—thus alienating those who may not fully align with their views. This binary thinking can create an environment where constructive dialogue is stifled, and the potential for collaboration across ideological divides is diminished. Democracies must cultivate a deep understanding of both internal and external threats, ensuring that their responses are informed and strategic rather than reactionary.

Andrés Tassara raises a critical concern regarding education and its role in democracy. When education shifts from fostering critical thinking to becoming a tool for indoctrination, the very foundation of democracy is at risk. An educated citizenry is essential for a functioning democracy, as it empowers individuals to engage thoughtfully in political discourse and make informed decisions. In the context of the woke generation, there is a risk that educational institutions may prioritize ideological conformity over critical inquiry, leading to a generation that may struggle to engage with diverse perspectives. This underscores the need for educational reform that prioritizes critical thinking, open dialogue, and the exploration of diverse viewpoints, rather than promoting a singular ideological narrative. Education should equip students with the skills to analyze information critically, question assumptions, and engage in respectful debate, fostering a culture of inquiry that is essential for a healthy democracy.

Gabriel Zaliasnik draws a parallel between cancel culture and historical acts of censorship, such as book burning. The suppression of dissenting voices, whether through social ostracism or institutional measures, poses a significant threat to the essence of a free society. Cancel culture can create an environment of fear where individuals hesitate to express their opinions, stifling open discourse and debate. In a healthy democracy, dissent is not only tolerated but celebrated as a vital component of public discourse. The woke generation's emphasis on social justice and accountability can sometimes lead to a climate where dissenting opinions are silenced, undermining the democratic principle of free expression. Silencing opposing viewpoints not only threatens the diversity of ideas but also risks creating an echo chamber that stifles innovation and critical thought. The danger lies in equating dissent with harm, leading to a culture where individuals may feel compelled to self-censor rather than engage in meaningful dialogue.

The interplay between the challenges posed by the woke generation and the broader threats to democracy highlights the need for a balanced approach. While the pursuit of social justice and equity is essential, it must be pursued in a manner that respects the principles of democratic engagement and open dialogue. This requires a commitment to fostering a culture where differing opinions can be expressed and debated without fear of retribution. The challenge is to create spaces for constructive dialogue that allow for the expression of diverse viewpoints while also addressing legitimate grievances related to social justice.

Moreover, these challenges highlight the importance of civic engagement and participation. Citizens must be encouraged to actively participate in the democratic process, not only by voting but also by engaging in community discussions, advocating for their beliefs, and holding their leaders accountable. A robust civil society, characterized by active participation and engagement, can serve as a bulwark against the encroachment of authoritarianism and the erosion of democratic norms. Civic education plays a crucial role in this process, equipping individuals with the knowledge and skills necessary to navigate the complexities of democratic governance and to engage effectively in public discourse.

In addition, the role of social media in shaping public opinion cannot be overlooked. While social media platforms can facilitate the rapid dissemination of information and mobilize support for social causes, they can also contribute to the spread of misinformation and exacerbate polarization. The algorithms that govern these platforms often prioritize sensational content, which can distort public discourse and create echo chambers. Democracies must find ways to promote media literacy and critical thinking skills among citizens, enabling them to navigate the digital landscape more effectively and discern credible information from misinformation.

There is a need for a call to action for democracies worldwide. They remind us that the health of democracy is not solely the responsibility of political leaders but also of the citizenry. By fostering a culture of critical inquiry, protecting dissent, and remaining vigilant against the forces that seek to undermine democratic principles, societies can build resilience against the challenges of the 21st century. The survival of democracy depends on the collective commitment to uphold its values, ensuring that it remains a vibrant and dynamic system that reflects the will and aspirations of its people.

There is a pressing need for a call to action for democracies worldwide. In recent years, we have witnessed a rise in authoritarianism, populism, and attacks on democratic institutions in various parts of the world. These challenges remind us that the health of democracy is not solely the responsibility of political leaders but also of the citizenry. It is crucial for individuals to actively engage in the democratic process, uphold democratic values, and defend the principles that underpin our societies.

One of the key ways in which citizens can contribute to the strength of democracy is by fostering a culture of critical inquiry. This involves questioning authority, challenging assumptions, and seeking out diverse perspectives. By encouraging open and honest dialogue, individuals can help to hold their leaders accountable and ensure that decisions are made in the best interests of the people. Critical inquiry also helps to guard against the spread of misinformation and propaganda, which can undermine the foundations of democracy.

Protecting dissent is another essential aspect of safeguarding democracy. Dissent is a fundamental right in a democratic society, allowing individuals to voice their opinions, express their grievances, and advocate for change. When dissent is suppressed or punished, it weakens the democratic fabric and stifles the diversity of thought that is essential for a thriving democracy. It is crucial for citizens to stand up for the rights of dissenters and defend their freedom of expression, even when their views may be unpopular or controversial.

Vigilance is also key in defending democracy against the forces that seek to undermine its principles. Authoritarian leaders, extremist groups, and foreign actors may attempt to erode democratic norms, manipulate elections, or sow division within societies. It is essential for citizens to remain vigilant against these threats, to be informed about the challenges facing democracy, and to actively resist attempts to subvert the democratic process. By staying alert and engaged, individuals can help to build resilience against the challenges of the 21st century.

Ultimately, the survival of democracy depends on the collective commitment of citizens to uphold its values. Democracy is not a static system but a dynamic one that requires constant care and attention. It is up to each and every one of us to ensure that democracy remains a vibrant and inclusive system that reflects the will and aspirations of its people. By fostering a culture of critical inquiry, protecting dissent, and remaining vigilant against threats, we can help to strengthen democracy and ensure that it continues to thrive for generations to come.

Ultimately, the interplay between the challenges posed by the woke generation and the broader threats to democracy underscores the need for a nuanced approach to social change. Democracies must navigate the complexities of addressing social injustices while preserving the foundational principles of free expression, critical inquiry, and open dialogue. Only through such commitments can democracies hope to thrive in an increasingly complex and hostile world, ensuring that the quest for justice does not come at the expense of the very freedoms that define democratic societies.

As democracies move forward, it is essential to recognize that the pursuit of social justice and the protection of democratic values are not mutually exclusive. Rather, they can be complementary goals that enhance the overall health of society. Engaging in open dialogue about social issues, while also upholding the principles of free expression and critical inquiry, can lead to more informed and equitable solutions.

In this context, fostering an environment where diverse perspectives are welcomed and debated is crucial. This involves not only protecting the rights of individuals to express dissenting opinions but also encouraging a culture of empathy and understanding. By promoting respectful dialogue and active listening, democracies can bridge divides and foster a sense of community that transcends ideological differences.

Furthermore, the role of leadership in navigating these challenges cannot be overstated. Leaders must model the values of democratic engagement, demonstrating a commitment to inclusivity, transparency, and accountability. They should encourage open dialogue and create spaces for citizens to voice their concerns and ideas. By fostering a culture of trust and collaboration, leaders can help to mitigate the polarization that often characterizes contemporary political discourse.

In summary, the challenges faced by democracies in the 21st century are complex and multifaceted, particularly in the context of the woke generation. By embracing the principles of critical inquiry, protecting dissent, and fostering civic engagement, democracies can navigate these challenges while remaining true to their foundational values. The survival of democracy depends on the collective efforts of citizens, leaders, and institutions to uphold the ideals of freedom, equality, and justice. Only through a shared commitment to these principles can democracies hope to thrive and adapt in an ever-changing world, ensuring that the quest for social justice enhances rather than undermines the very freedoms that define democratic societies.

The quotes from professors J.J. Brunner, Michael Ehrlich, Andrés Tassara, and Gabriel Zaliasnik shed light on the challenges faced by democracies in the 21st century, especially in the wake of the rise of the so-called "woke generation." This term, which has gained popularity in recent years, refers to a heightened awareness of social injustices and a commitment to addressing systemic inequalities.

One of the key challenges highlighted by these quotes is the need for democracies to adapt to the changing social and political landscape. As Professor Brunner points out, the "woke generation" is demanding a more inclusive and equitable society, one that addresses the historical injustices that have marginalized certain groups. This presents a challenge for democracies, which must find ways to respond to these demands while also upholding the principles of democracy and protecting the rights of all citizens.

Professor Ehrlich's quote underscores the importance of education in addressing these challenges. In order to create a more just and equitable society, individuals must be educated about the systemic inequalities that exist and empowered to take action to address them. This highlights the role that education plays in shaping the values and beliefs of the "woke generation" and in driving social change.

Andrés Tassara's quote speaks to the need for democracies to engage with diverse perspectives and voices in order to address the complex challenges of the 21st century. In a world that is increasingly interconnected, democracies must be able to navigate the tensions that arise from differing viewpoints and find ways to build consensus and collaboration across diverse communities.

Finally, Gabriel Zaliasnik's quote highlights the importance of upholding the rule of law and protecting the rights of all individuals, even in the face of social upheaval. Democracies must find ways to balance the demands of the "woke generation" with the need to uphold the principles of democracy and protect the rights of all citizens.

Many politicians and intellectuals underscore the challenges faced by democracies in the 21st century, particularly in the context of the rise of the "woke generation." These challenges require democracies to adapt to changing social and political dynamics, prioritize education and dialogue, engage with diverse perspectives, and uphold the rule of law. By addressing these challenges head-on, democracies can work towards creating a more just and equitable society for all.

Professors and politicians have been shed light on the challenges faced by democracies in the 21st century, especially in the wake of the rise of the so-called "woke generation." This term, which has gained popularity in recent years, refers to a heightened awareness of social injustices and a commitment to addressing systemic inequalities.

One of the key challenges highlighted by these quotes is the need for democracies to adapt to the changing social and political landscape. As Professor Brunner points out, the "woke generation" is demanding a more inclusive and equitable society, one that addresses the historical injustices that have marginalized certain groups. This presents a challenge for democracies, which must find ways to respond to these demands while also upholding the principles of democracy and protecting the rights of all citizens.

Professor Ehrlich's quote underscores the importance of education in addressing these challenges. In order to create a more just and equitable society, individuals must be educated about the systemic inequalities that exist and empowered to take action to address them. This highlights the role that education plays in shaping the values and beliefs of the "woke generation" and in driving social change.

Andrés Tassara's quote speaks to the need for democracies to engage with diverse perspectives and voices in order to address the complex challenges of the 21st century. In a world that is increasingly interconnected, democracies must be able to navigate the tensions that arise from differing viewpoints and find ways to build consensus and collaboration across diverse communities.

Finally, Gabriel Zaliasnik's quote highlights the importance of upholding the rule of law and protecting the rights of all individuals, even in the face of social upheaval. Democracies must find ways to balance the demands of the "woke generation" with the need to uphold the principles of democracy and protect the rights of all citizens.

The challenges faced by democracies in the 21st century, particularly in the context of the rise of the "woke generation." These challenges require democracies to adapt to changing social and political dynamics, prioritize education and dialogue, engage with diverse perspectives, and uphold the rule of law. By addressing these challenges head-on, democracies can work towards creating a more just and equitable society for all.

Double standards in the treatment of Israel by international bodies represent a significant challenge for the Jewish state and its democratic values. These discrepancies often manifest in the form of disproportionate criticism, biased resolutions, and a lack of accountability for those who perpetrate violence against Israel. Such treatment not only undermines Israel's legitimacy but also poses broader implications for the principles of democracy and justice on the global stage.

The Context of Double Standards

International organizations, including the United Nations and various human rights groups, have frequently been accused of applying double standards when addressing issues related to Israel. Resolutions condemning Israel for its actions in the context of the Israeli-Palestinian conflict often outnumber those addressing human rights violations by other nations, including those with egregious records of oppression and violence. This selective scrutiny can create a narrative that delegitimizes Israel's right to defend itself and undermines its sovereignty.

Implications for Democracy

Senator Jaime Quintana's assertion that "if democracies do not wake up to the double standards of international organizations, they will find themselves isolated in their own defense" underscores the urgent need for democratic nations to recognize and respond to these biases. When international bodies fail to uphold consistent standards of justice and accountability, they risk alienating democratic states that strive to adhere to the rule of law and human rights. This isolation can weaken the resolve of democracies to defend their values and interests, particularly when they are unjustly targeted.

The Ideological Battle

The issue of double standards is not merely a diplomatic concern; it is part of a broader ideological battle that democracies face today. As Guillermo Holzman notes, "the global battle today is not just military; it is ideological, fought in classrooms, in the media, and in institutions." The narratives surrounding Israel often extend beyond the political realm, influencing public opinion and educational discourse. By framing Israel as an aggressor while ignoring the complexities of the conflict, these narratives can foster anti-Semitism and delegitimize the Jewish state's right to exist.

The Role of Education and Media

In this ideological struggle, education and media play crucial roles. Educational institutions must promote critical thinking and a nuanced understanding of historical and contemporary issues, including the Israeli-Palestinian conflict. By providing students with a comprehensive view that includes diverse perspectives, democracies can combat the simplistic narratives that often dominate public discourse. Similarly, media outlets have a responsibility to report on the complexities of the situation in a balanced manner, avoiding sensationalism that can perpetuate bias and misunderstanding.

A Call for Accountability

To address the issue of double standards, democracies must advocate for reforms within international organizations that promote fairness and accountability. This includes calling out bias in resolutions and ensuring that all nations are held to the same standards regarding human rights and conflict resolution. By standing together against unjust treatment of Israel, democratic nations can reinforce their commitment to universal principles of justice and equality.

Conclusion

The challenge of double standards against Israel is emblematic of broader issues facing democracies today. As nations navigate the complexities of international relations, they must remain vigilant against biases that threaten their legitimacy and values. By fostering a culture of accountability, promoting education that encourages critical inquiry, and engaging in constructive dialogue, democracies can combat the forces that seek to undermine their principles.

Ultimately, the survival of democratic values in the face of double standards requires a collective commitment to uphold justice and equality for all nations. By addressing these challenges head-on, democracies can ensure that they remain resilient and responsive to the needs of their citizens, while also standing in solidarity with those who face unjust treatment on the global stage.

Israel a challenge to survive

Gabriel Silber, a prominent figure in Chilean politics, once stated, "A nation that abandons its historical identity will eventually abandon its moral compass." These words ring true, not only for Chile but for every country. Our history shapes our present and future, and by disregarding our past, we risk losing our sense of right and wrong. This is especially evident in times of conflict, where decisions are often based on expediency rather than morality.

Former Chilean Congressman, Professor Marco Antonio Núñez Lozano echoes Silber's sentiment, emphasizing the need for accountability from international institutions. "We must demand accountability from the UN and other institutions that selectively apply justice," stated Núñez Lozano. In a world where justice is often seen as subjective and biased, it is essential to hold those in positions of power accountable for their actions. This not only ensures fairness but also promotes transparency and strengthens trust in international organizations.

Sharren Haskel, a member of the Israeli Knesset, speaks about the ongoing conflict in the Middle East and the role of her country in defending the values of the free world. "Israel is not just defending itself – it is defending the values of the free world against those who seek to dismantle them," she said. Israel has faced numerous security threats since its inception, and yet, it has managed to preserve its democratic and liberal values. Haskel's words highlight the resilience and determination of the Israeli people who refuse to succumb to external pressures and threats.

Netanya's Mayor, a city in Israel, also shares a similar sentiment. "Security is not just about military strength – it is about preserving the fabric of our democratic society." As a leader responsible for the safety and well-being of her citizens, she understands that security is not just about physical protection but also about safeguarding the core values of a society. Without these values, a nation risks losing its identity and unity, which are crucial for its survival.

Ron Brummer, a former Israeli security official, stresses the need for a comprehensive approach to conflict resolution. "A temporary ceasefire without dismantling terrorist infrastructure is just an opportunity for rearmament." This statement highlights the importance of addressing the root causes of conflict rather than just the symptoms. A temporary solution may provide temporary relief, but without addressing the underlying issues, the conflict is likely to resurface in the future.

In conclusion, the voices of Gabriel Silber, Marco Antonio Núñez Lozano, Sharren Haskel, Netanya's Mayor, and Ron Brummer serve as a reminder that a nation's identity, values, and society must be preserved and protected against external threats. Their words and actions demonstrate the importance of accountability, resilience, and a holistic approach when dealing with conflicts. As we move forward, let us not forget our past, but learn from it and safeguard our present and future.

A nation's historical identity is deeply intertwined with its moral compass. Gabriel Silber's statement that "a nation that abandons its historical identity will eventually abandon its moral compass" holds true in many contexts, including the ongoing conflict in Israel. As former Deputy Marco Antonio Núñez Lozano suggests, accountability is crucial in ensuring that justice is applied consistently and fairly by institutions such as the UN.

In the face of threats to its values and security, Israel has consistently defended itself and the principles of the free world. Sharren Haskel's assertion that Israel is not just defending itself, but also the values of the free world, highlights the importance of standing firm against those who seek to dismantle these values. The Mayor of Netanya emphasizes that security is not just about military strength, but also about preserving the democratic fabric of society.

Ron Brummer's warning that a temporary ceasefire without dismantling terrorist infrastructure only allows for rearmament underscores the need for a comprehensive approach to security. The IDF, as Kaplan Rony points out, operates under one of the strictest ethical codes in the world, yet faces intense scrutiny internationally.

David Ben-Gurion's belief in miracles as a prerequisite for realism in Israel reflects the country's history of overcoming seemingly insurmountable challenges. Golda Meir's poignant statement that peace will come when the Arabs love their children more than they hate Israel speaks to the deep-rooted complexities of the conflict.

In conclusion, the statements of these Israeli leaders and officials highlight the multifaceted nature of the conflict in Israel and the importance of upholding historical identity, moral values, and security in the pursuit of peace. As the country continues to navigate these challenges, it is essential to remain vigilant, accountable, and committed to defending the values that underpin a democratic society.

**

DEFENDING DEMOCRACY AGAINST TERRORISM

INTRODUCTION: THE MORAL CHALLENGE OF DEMOCRATIC DEFENSE

Democracy is built on principles of freedom, human rights, and the rule of law. However, these same principles can become vulnerabilities when faced with adversaries who reject them outright. Nowhere is this contradiction more evident than in Israel, a nation that must defend itself against terrorism while upholding its democratic and ethical values.

The Israel Defense Forces (IDF) operate under one of the strictest ethical codes in the world, yet Israel is the most scrutinized army internationally. **Rony Kaplan** highlights this paradox: *"The IDF operates under one of the strictest ethical codes in the world—yet it is the most scrutinized army internationally."* While authoritarian regimes eliminate threats without regard for human rights, democratic nations like Israel are expected to fight under constraints that their enemies do not respect.

Despite its small size and constant threats, Israel has survived and thrived, proving that a democracy can defend itself without losing its moral compass. However, the challenges continue to mount, as terrorist organizations, backed by hostile states, manipulate international law, public perception, and even humanitarian institutions to undermine Israel's right to self-defense.

This chapter examines Israel's struggle to balance security with democratic ideals, highlighting how its experience serves as a warning—and a lesson—for other democracies confronting terrorism.

THE STRUGGLE FOR FREEDOM AND SECURITY

The survival of a democracy is not guaranteed—it must be actively defended. As **Menachem Begin** warned: *"A nation that does not stand for its freedom will not have a future."* Since its inception, Israel has been forced to fight multiple wars and defend itself against continuous acts of terrorism.

One of the great paradoxes of democratic defense is that, unlike its enemies, a democracy must justify its actions at every turn. Terrorist organizations like Hamas and Hezbollah intentionally blur the line between combatants and civilians, forcing Israel to make impossible choices: should it strike a military target knowing terrorists are using human shields, or should it hold back and risk Israeli lives? The world rarely asks these questions of Israel's enemies. Instead, international organizations and media outlets often rush to condemn Israel, ignoring the fact that it fights against groups that openly call for genocide.

Yitzhak Rabin encapsulated this reality with his famous statement: *"We must fight terrorism as if there were no peace process, and pursue peace as if there were no terrorism."* This philosophy reflects the dual responsibility of Israel: it must remain open to peaceful solutions while never underestimating the threats posed by those who reject coexistence.

Einat Wilf, a scholar and former Knesset member, explains that *"Democracies lose wars when they choose not to win them."* Her observation is particularly relevant when examining how Israel is often pressured into restraint by international actors who fail to recognize the existential nature of its struggle. Wilf argues that many in the West misunderstand the fundamental nature of the conflict, mistakenly believing that concessions will lead to peace, when in reality, they are often perceived as weakness by Israel's enemies.

Similarly, **Haviv Gur** points out that *"Israel's greatest challenge is not only the military one, but the battle over* *narrative—the effort to convince the world that it has a right to defend itself."* This struggle over perception is one of the most significant challenges modern democracies face when dealing with terrorism.

Yitzhak Rabin's famous statement encapsulates the complex reality that Israel faces in its ongoing struggle against terrorism while simultaneously striving for peace. Rabin understood that Israel must navigate a delicate balance between fighting terrorism with all its might and remaining committed to pursuing peaceful solutions. This dual responsibility reflects the unique challenges that Israel faces as a nation constantly under threat from those who reject coexistence.

Einat Wilf's observation that "Democracies lose wars when they choose not to win them" highlights the importance of Israel's ability to defend itself against terrorist threats. The pressure from international actors to show restraint can often be misguided, as it fails to recognize the existential nature of Israel's struggle. Concessions made in the name of peace can be perceived as weakness by Israel's enemies, further complicating the already complex situation.

Haviv Gur's insight into the battle over narrative underscores the importance of perception in the fight against terrorism. Israel not only faces a military challenge but also a battle to convince the world of its right to defend itself. The struggle to shape the narrative surrounding Israel's actions is crucial in garnering support and understanding from the international community.

In conclusion, Yitzhak Rabin's philosophy of fighting terrorism while pursuing peace reflects the dual responsibility that Israel must uphold. The nation must remain vigilant in its fight against terrorism while also remaining open to peaceful solutions. The challenges of navigating international pressure, perceptions, and narratives further complicate Israel's struggle, highlighting the need for a nuanced and strategic approach to addressing the ongoing conflict.

THE PRICE OF MORAL CLARITY IN WAR

Israel has always understood that its struggle is not merely a military one but a battle for legitimacy in the court of global opinion. **Golda Meir** captured this moral dilemma when she stated: *"Peace will come when the Arabs love their children more than they hate us."* Her words underscore the asymmetry of the conflict: Israel fights to protect its civilians, while terrorist organizations like Hamas and Hezbollah deliberately endanger their own people to manipulate international perception.

As **Einat Wilf** has further explained, *"The greatest injustice done to the Palestinian people is to encourage them to believe they do not need to accept defeat."* She highlights how Palestinian leadership has continually rejected peace plans, perpetuating conflict and suffering among their own people. The refusal to recognize Israel's legitimacy and the promotion of eternal victimhood have prevented any real progress toward coexistence.

The reality is that Israel operates under uniquely restrictive conditions. **Haviv Gur** has noted that *"No other country in the world would tolerate the kind of threats that Israel faces daily—yet it is the one constantly being asked to show restraint."* This expectation places Israel in an impossible position: either act decisively and face international condemnation, or do nothing and allow its citizens to suffer.

Israel has always been acutely aware that its struggle for survival is not just a military one, but also a battle for legitimacy in the court of global opinion. Former Israeli Prime Minister Golda Meir succinctly captured this moral dilemma when she famously stated, "Peace will come when the Arabs love their children more than they hate us." This statement underscores the stark asymmetry of the conflict: Israel is fighting to protect its civilians, while terrorist organizations like Hamas and Hezbollah deliberately endanger their own people in order to manipulate international perception.

In her analysis, Einat Wilf points out that one of the greatest injustices done to the Palestinian people is the encouragement of a belief that they do not need to accept defeat. This refusal to acknowledge Israel's right to exist and the perpetuation of a narrative of eternal victimhood have only served to prolong the conflict and exacerbate the suffering of the Palestinian people. The rejection of numerous peace plans by Palestinian leadership has further hindered any progress towards a lasting resolution to the conflict.

Israel operates under uniquely challenging circumstances, as Haviv Gur has observed. The country faces daily threats to its security that no other nation would tolerate, yet it is constantly being asked to show restraint in its response. This double standard places Israel in an impossible position, where it must choose between taking decisive action to protect its citizens and risking international condemnation, or refraining from action and allowing its people to continue to suffer.

Israel's struggle for legitimacy in the global arena is a complex and ongoing battle. The country faces not only military threats from terrorist organizations, but also a concerted effort to delegitimize its very existence. Despite these challenges, Israel remains committed to defending its citizens and pursuing peace, even in the face of relentless hostility and unfair criticism. It is imperative for the international community to recognize the unique challenges faced by Israel and to support its right to self-defense and security.

ISRAEL AS A MODEL OF RESILIENCE

Despite relentless attacks and ongoing delegitimization efforts, Israel has not only survived but thrived. The words of **David Ben-Gurion**, the nation's founding father, still resonate today: *"In Israel, to be a realist, you must believe in miracles."*

Israel's ability to balance democracy with the realities of war is a model for other nations confronting terrorism. Unlike many authoritarian regimes that deal with threats through mass suppression, Israel has developed legal and military frameworks that allow it to fight effectively while maintaining the highest ethical standards. The IDF's "Purity of Arms" doctrine, which mandates that soldiers minimize harm to civilians even in combat situations, is a testament to Israel's commitment to moral warfare.

Israel, a nation born out of struggle and conflict, has faced relentless attacks and ongoing delegitimization efforts since its establishment in 1948. Despite these challenges, Israel has not only survived but thrived, becoming a beacon of democracy and innovation in the Middle East. The words of David Ben-Gurion, the nation's founding father, still resonate today: "In Israel, to be a realist, you must believe in miracles."

One of the key factors in Israel's resilience is its ability to balance democracy with the realities of war. Unlike many authoritarian regimes that deal with threats through mass suppression and human rights abuses, Israel has developed legal and military frameworks that allow it to fight effectively while maintaining the highest ethical standards. The Israel Defense Forces (IDF) follow the "Purity of Arms" doctrine, which mandates that soldiers minimize harm to civilians even in combat situations. This commitment to moral warfare sets Israel apart from many other nations facing similar security challenges.

Israel's ability to thrive in the face of adversity can also be attributed to its culture of innovation and entrepreneurship. Despite being a small country with limited natural resources, Israel has become a global leader in technology, agriculture, and healthcare. Israeli startups and companies are at the forefront of cutting-edge technologies such as cybersecurity, artificial intelligence, and renewable energy. This spirit of innovation has not only driven Israel's economic growth but has also strengthened its security by providing the IDF with advanced tools and capabilities.

Furthermore, Israel's strong sense of national identity and unity has played a crucial role in its survival and success. Despite being a diverse society with a complex history, Israelis have shown a remarkable ability to come together in times of crisis and work towards a common goal. This sense of solidarity has enabled Israel to overcome numerous challenges, from wars and terrorist attacks to economic downturns and political turmoil.

Israel's ability to survive and thrive despite relentless attacks and ongoing delegitimization efforts is a testament to its resilience, innovation, and unity. By balancing democracy with the realities of war, upholding ethical standards in its military operations, fostering a culture of innovation, and maintaining a strong sense of national identity, Israel has not only defied the odds but has emerged as a model for other nations confronting terrorism and conflict. As David Ben-Gurion once said, in Israel, to be a realist, you must believe in miracles – and indeed, Israel's ability to overcome adversity and achieve success can only be described as miraculous.

CONCLUSION: DEMOCRACY'S STRENGTH IN THE FACE OF TERROR

Democracies must not allow their moral standards to become weaknesses exploited by those who seek their destruction. The defense of democracy requires strength, vigilance, and an unyielding commitment to truth. Israel's experience is a testament to this balance, proving that a nation can stand firm against terror while upholding the values that define it.

As history has shown, the greatest threat to democracies is not just external enemies but the internal hesitation to defend their principles. In the words of **Menachem Begin**, "A *nation that does not stand for its freedom will not have a future."* The time has come for the free world to stand with Israel—not only in solidarity but in recognition that its fight is the fight of every democracy that refuses to be silenced by terror.

Israel's lessons in counterterrorism, law, and ethics should serve as a blueprint for other nations facing the growing threat of radicalism. If democracies wish to survive, they must be willing to defend themselves—not only on the battlefield but in the war of ideas. As **Einat Wilf** has warned, *"A democracy that is unwilling to win is one that has already lost."*

The battle for democracy is not just about survival—it is about the willingness to fight for the values that define it.

**

PROGRESSIVE IN DANGER: THE FRAGILITY OF DEMOCRACY

INTRODUCTION: THE TEST OF DEMOCRACIES

Democracy is often viewed as an unshakable system, an

inevitability in the modern world. However, history has repeatedly shown that democratic institutions are fragile, vulnerable to internal decay and external threats. The greatest danger to democracies is not necessarily military conquest, but rather the slow erosion of democratic principles from within.

Levi Eshkol recognized this when he stated: *"A nation is not tested by how it builds, but by how it defends what it has built."* His words highlight the reality that progress and stability are not permanent achievements; they must be actively defended. If a democracy does not reinforce its core values and institutions, it risks becoming complacent and ultimately vulnerable to forces that seek its destruction.

In recent years, democracies across the world have faced increasing challenges from populism, radical ideologies, and external pressures from authoritarian regimes. As **Felipe González** warned: *"Western democracies have become too comfortable with their freedoms—they forget how fragile they really are."* This complacency has allowed illiberal movements to gain traction, often using the very mechanisms of democracy to weaken it from within.

This chapter explores the growing threats to progressive democracies, analyzing how extremism, populism, and moral relativism have created an environment in which the very foundations of liberal governance are at risk.

In recent years, progressive democracies around the world have faced an increasing number of threats that challenge the very core principles of liberal governance. This chapter delves into the various factors that have contributed to this growing instability, including extremism, populism, and moral relativism. Through the perspectives of former leaders such as Felipe Gonzales, Ricardo Lagos, Jaime Quintana, and Marco Antonio Núñez Lozano, we gain insight into the challenges facing modern democracies and the urgent need for action to protect the values of freedom, equality, and justice.

Extremism has emerged as a significant threat to progressive democracies, with radical ideologies gaining traction and undermining the foundations of liberal governance. As Felipe Gonzales, former Prime Minister of Spain, notes, extremist movements have exploited social divisions and economic inequalities to sow discord and promote their dangerous agendas. From far-right nationalist groups to violent extremist organizations, these movements pose a direct threat to the principles of democracy and human rights.

Populism has also played a significant role in eroding the

foundations of progressive democracies. Ricardo Lagos, former President of Chile, highlights how populist leaders have capitalized on public discontent and fear to advance their own political agendas. By appealing to emotions rather than reason, populists have undermined the institutions and norms that are essential for a functioning democracy. Their divisive rhetoric and disregard for democratic norms have fueled polarization and undermined trust in democratic institutions.

Moral relativism further complicates the challenges facing progressive democracies, as it erodes the shared values and principles that underpin liberal governance. Jaime Quintana, a prominent political figure in Chile, warns of the dangers of moral relativism, which blurs the lines between right and wrong and undermines the moral foundations of society. In a world where truth is increasingly subjective and facts are dismissed as "fake news," the very concept of objective reality is called into question, making it difficult to uphold the principles of democracy and justice.

Marco Antonio Núñez Lozano, a respected academic and political analyst, emphasizes the urgent need for action to address these threats to progressive democracies. He calls for a renewed commitment to defending the values of freedom, equality, and justice that are essential for a functioning democracy. By promoting dialogue, fostering understanding, and upholding the rule of law, we can counter the forces of extremism, populism, and moral relativism that threaten to undermine the very foundations of liberal governance.

In conclusion, the growing threats to progressive democracies require a concerted effort to defend the values and principles that are essential for a functioning democracy. By recognizing the dangers of extremism, populism, and moral relativism, and taking action to address these challenges, we can safeguard the future of liberal governance and ensure that democracy remains a beacon of hope and progress for all.

THE DEMOCRATIC PARADOX: FREEDOM AS A WEAKNESS?

One of the great ironies of democracy is that it allows space for voices that actively seek its destruction. In open societies, radical ideologies—whether from the far left or far right—can infiltrate political discourse, exploit freedoms, and undermine democratic structures from within.

Shimon Peres warned of this danger when he said:

"Democracy is not just about voting—it is about protecting the integrity of institutions against populism and extremism." His insight is particularly relevant today, as many democracies struggle against rising political polarization, the manipulation of democratic institutions, and the deliberate spread of misinformation designed to erode trust in governance.

The fundamental problem is that democracies, in their desire to remain tolerant and open, often fail to recognize when they are being subverted. Extremist movements, whether religious, ideological, or nationalist, understand that democratic systems are slow-moving, preferring compromise over confrontation. By the time a democracy reacts, it is often too late—the damage has already been done.

Willy Brandt famously stated: *"Those who forget history are doomed to repeat its tragedies."* This warning remains urgent in a time when many people, particularly in the West, believe that democracy is an irreversible historical achievement rather than a delicate system that must be actively protected. The collapse of past democracies—whether in the Weimar Republic, Chile in 1973, or Venezuela in recent decades—should serve as stark reminders that democratic regression is always a possibility.

One of the great ironies of democracy is that it provides a platform for voices that seek to undermine it. In open societies, radical ideologies from both the far left and far right can exploit freedoms and manipulate political discourse to weaken democratic structures from within. This poses a significant threat to the integrity of democratic institutions and the stability of society as a whole.

Shimon Peres rightly pointed out that democracy is not just about voting, but also about safeguarding the integrity of institutions against populism and extremism. This is especially relevant in today's political climate, where many democracies are grappling with increasing polarization, the manipulation of democratic processes, and the deliberate spread of misinformation to sow distrust in governance.

The core issue lies in the fact that democracies, in their commitment to tolerance and openness, often fail to recognize when they are being subverted. Extremist movements, whether driven by religious, ideological, or nationalist motives, understand that democratic systems are inherently slow-moving and prone to compromise. By the time the threat is identified, the damage has often already been done.

As Willy Brandt wisely observed, those who forget history are doomed to repeat its tragedies. It is crucial for us to remember that democracy is not a guaranteed outcome of history, but a fragile system that requires active protection and vigilance. The collapse of past democracies serves as a stark reminder that democratic regression is a real and present danger that must be taken seriously.

In conclusion, it is imperative for us to recognize the threat posed by voices that seek to undermine democracy from within. We must remain vigilant against extremist ideologies that exploit the freedoms of open societies to erode democratic institutions. By actively protecting the integrity of our democratic systems, we can ensure that the principles of democracy continue to thrive and endure for generations to come.

**

PROGRESSIVE IN DANGER: DEMOCRACY UNDER SIEGE

INTRODUCTION: THE PARADOX OF DEMOCRATIC VULNERABILITY

Democracy, once seen as the pinnacle of human governance, is now under siege from multiple fronts—external adversaries, internal polarization, and the manipulation of democratic values by those who seek its downfall.

Eduardo Frei Ruiz-Tagle warns: *"Chile has always stood with democratic values, but we must not allow those values to be twisted against us."* His statement reflects a broader challenge facing democracies worldwide: the very freedoms that define them—open discourse, legal protections, and institutional checks and balances—are often exploited by those who reject democratic principles.

Democracies are bound by rules, ethical standards, and due process. Their enemies—be they terrorist organizations, authoritarian regimes, or radical movements—are not. This asymmetry creates a dangerous paradox: democracies, in their commitment to human rights, can become

The Risk of the left....

Kidnapping is a heinous crime that has plagued societies for centuries. It is a terrifying act that can have devastating consequences for the victim and their loved ones. In recent years, kidnapping has also been used as a terror tool by extremist groups to instill fear and exert control over populations. This despicable tactic is often promoted by so-called progressive individuals who claim to be advocating for social justice and equality.

The use of kidnapping as a terror tool is a cowardly and reprehensible act that goes against the very principles of humanity. It is a violation of basic human rights and a blatant disregard for the sanctity of life. Those who engage in such acts are not progressive or revolutionary, but rather criminals who seek to spread fear and chaos.

Unfortunately, there are individuals who claim to be progressive and yet support or justify the use of kidnapping as a means to achieve their goals. They may argue that kidnapping is a necessary evil in the fight against oppression or injustice. However, this argument is deeply flawed and dangerous. Resorting to violence and terror only serves to perpetuate a cycle of hatred and conflict, leading to further suffering and harm.

It is important for society to condemn and reject the use of kidnapping as a terror tool, regardless of the perpetrators' motives or beliefs. We must stand united against such acts of violence and work towards peaceful and constructive solutions to address social injustices and inequalities.

In conclusion, kidnapping as a terror tool is a despicable crime that has no place in a civilized society. It is a violation of human rights and a threat to the safety and security of individuals. Those who promote or support such acts are not progressive or revolutionary, but rather misguided individuals who have lost sight of the true values of justice and compassion. It is imperative that we stand together against kidnapping and all forms of violence, and work towards a more peaceful and just world for all.

THE GLOBAL STRUGGLE: DEMOCRACY AGAINST TERRORISM

INTRODUCTION: A SHARED RESPONSIBILITY

Terrorism is not just a threat to individual nations—it is a challenge to the very foundations of democracy, freedom, and human dignity. The recent surge in global terrorist activity, particularly the atrocities committed by Hamas and other extremist groups, has made it clear that this is not just Israel's battle. As **President Javier Milei** rightly asserts: *"The fight against terrorism is not just Israel's fight—it is the fight of all democracies that value freedom."*

Democracies that fail to recognize this reality risk repeating the mistakes of history—ignoring threats until they become existential crises. As the **President of Germany** warns: *"Our commitment to Israel's security is not negotiable. A world that allows antisemitism to thrive is a world that has learned nothing from history."*

This chapter explores how democratic leaders across the world are recognizing the shared responsibility of confronting terrorism, defending freedom, and ensuring that history's darkest chapters do not repeat themselves.

THE THREAT OF TERRORISM: A UNIVERSAL CHALLENGE

Terrorist organizations do not operate in a vacuum. They thrive in environments where extremism is tolerated, where democratic nations hesitate to take decisive action, and where the world fails to distinguish between aggressor and victim.

Hamas, for example, has turned Gaza into a launching pad for terrorism, not a place for prosperity. **Nayib Bukele**, the President of El Salvador, stated unequivocally: *"The best thing that can happen to the Palestinian people is the disappearance of Hamas, a group that has only brought destruction and suffering."* His words reflect an understanding that groups like Hamas do not represent the true interests of the Palestinian people; rather, they use them as human shields and political pawns.

Likewise, the **President of Paraguay** makes it clear that supporting Israel in its battle against terror is not just a matter of diplomacy but of fundamental principles: *"We stand with Israel not just as a matter of diplomacy, but because we recognize the right of every nation to defend itself against terror."*

The threat of terrorism extends beyond Israel. Latin America, Europe, and even the United States have all seen how extremist ideologies infiltrate societies, radicalizing individuals and destabilizing communities. The failure to address these threats decisively has led to tragedies in Buenos Aires, Madrid, London, and New York.

THE MORAL CLARITY OF DEFENDING DEMOCRACY

One of the most damaging trends in the modern world is the

moral relativism that equates democratic nations with terrorist groups, treating them as if they are equally culpable. Israel, for instance, is regularly accused of "disproportionate force" when responding to attacks, while Hamas's indiscriminate rocket fire, hostage-taking, and civilian massacres are downplayed or ignored.

This double standard is not only hypocritical—it is dangerous. It emboldens terrorist organizations, discourages democracies from taking necessary action, and erodes the global fight against extremism.

The **President of Germany** makes a crucial point: *"Our commitment to Israel's security is not negotiable."* Germany, with its historical responsibility, understands that allowing antisemitism to flourish leads to dire consequences not just for Jews, but for the world as a whole.

President Javier Milei takes this further, arguing that the fight against terrorism is not a localized issue: *"The fight against terrorism is not just Israel's fight—it is the fight of all democracies that value freedom."* This highlights the importance of international cooperation, intelligence-sharing, and unified action against extremist threats.

THE ROLE OF LEADERSHIP IN PRESERVING DEMOCRACY

Strong leadership is essential in times of crisis. Democracies must recognize that weakness in the face of terror is an invitation for further aggression. This does not mean abandoning democratic values, but rather reinforcing them through decisive action.

- **Terrorists must be confronted, not appeased.** Any attempt to negotiate with groups like Hamas, Hezbollah, or ISIS without first dismantling their operational capabilities will only lead to further violence.
- **Democracies must not fear condemnation for defending themselves.** The international community often pressures Israel and other nations to "show restraint" while ignoring the brutality of the terrorists they fight. A nation's first responsibility is to protect its citizens.
- **The media and international organizations must be held accountable.** Misinformation and biased reporting have enabled terrorist narratives to spread, leading to misguided policy decisions and misplaced public sympathy for extremist causes.

The failure to act against terror today will only make the world more dangerous tomorrow.

CONCLUSION: A UNIFIED FRONT AGAINST TERRORISM

The leaders quoted in this chapter recognize that the battle against terrorism is not an isolated issue—it is a fundamental challenge for every democracy that values freedom, security, and human rights.

- **Nayib Bukele** calls out the real problem: *"The best thing that can happen to the Palestinian people is the disappearance of Hamas."*
- **President Javier Milei** frames it as a global struggle: *"The fight against terrorism is not just Israel's fight—it is the fight of all democracies that value freedom."*
- **The President of Paraguay** highlights the principle of national defense: *"We stand with Israel not just as a matter of diplomacy, but because we recognize the right of every nation to defend itself against terror."*
- **The President of Germany** emphasizes historical responsibility: *"A world that allows antisemitism to thrive is a world that has learned nothing from history."*

The free world must not remain passive. Democracies must recognize that their survival depends on their willingness to defend themselves—not just against traditional military threats, but against the ideological and political forces that enable terrorism to thrive.

This is not just about Israel. This is about the survival of democratic values in the 21st century. The choice is clear: stand firm against terror, or allow the forces of extremism to dictate the future.

A UNITED FRONT: DEFENDING DEMOCRACY AGAINST TERRORISM

INTRODUCTION: THE GLOBAL RESPONSIBILITY TO DEFEND FREEDOM

The survival of democracy is not a given—it is a responsibility. Around the world, democratic nations face growing threats from radical ideologies, terrorism, and external actors seeking to undermine their institutions. Nowhere is this struggle more evident than in Israel, a country that has been on the front lines of defending democracy for decades.

As the **President of the Czech Republic** rightly asserts: *"Standing with Israel means standing with democracy, law, and the right of a nation to protect its citizens."* His words reflect a broader truth: supporting Israel's right to self-defense is not just about supporting one country—it is about reinforcing the principle that democracies must have the ability to protect themselves against those who seek their destruction.

This chapter explores the moral and strategic necessity of

defending democracy in an era where terrorist organizations, radical ideologues, and authoritarian regimes seek to dismantle the very freedoms that democratic societies cherish.

THE DOUBLE STANDARD AGAINST DEMOCRACIES

Democratic nations are often held to impossible standards when it comes to warfare and self-defense. They are expected to follow strict ethical codes, abide by international law, and prioritize human rights—while their adversaries operate with impunity, disregarding every norm of civilized conflict.

Aviv Gur captures this double standard perfectly: *"Those who seek to dismantle Israel do not just oppose Zionism; they oppose the very idea that democracy has the right to defend itself."*

This is not merely a theoretical debate—it has real consequences. When Israel is condemned for defending its citizens against Hamas rocket attacks, while Hamas itself is not held accountable for targeting civilians, it emboldens terrorists worldwide. It signals that democracies will always be criticized for defending themselves, while extremists face no repercussions for their actions.

Zvy Hazklel reinforces this warning: *"History will not judge* *democracies for how they defended themselves—it will judge them for how they hesitated when faced with clear threats."* The failure to confront terrorism decisively today will only create a more dangerous world tomorrow.

ISRAEL AS A MODEL OF RESILIENCE

Israel's ability to withstand constant existential threats while maintaining its democratic framework is a lesson for all free nations. **Carlos Tapiero** emphasizes this reality: *"Israel's resilience in the face of adversity is a lesson for all democracies—security is not a privilege, it is a necessity."*

Unlike authoritarian regimes, which maintain stability through oppression and fear, Israel's democracy thrives despite ongoing conflict. This is not an accident—it is a testament to the strength of its people, institutions, and values.

Ron Brumer underscores the importance of a strong, decisive response to terrorism: *"The war against terrorism cannot be fought with weak rhetoric. It must be fought with strength, intelligence, and unwavering resolve."*

Israel does not merely survive; it defends itself proactively. It has developed one of the world's most sophisticated counterterrorism strategies, proving that democracies do not need to sacrifice their values in order to ensure security.

THE FAILURE OF PALESTINIAN LEADERSHIP AND THE MYTH OF PERPETUAL VICTIMHOOD

One of the most damaging narratives in global politics is the idea that the Palestinian leadership has been consistently willing to negotiate peace, only to be denied statehood by Israel. This is a falsehood that ignores a long history of rejectionism.

Einat Wilf exposes this deception: *"The Palestinian leadership has rejected every opportunity for statehood because their goal has never been to build a nation—it has always been to destroy one."*

From the 1947 UN Partition Plan to the 2000 Camp David Summit, Palestinian leaders have walked away from every serious offer for peace. Their refusal to accept a Jewish state, no matter the borders, is the fundamental reason the conflict persists.

Meanwhile, Israel has made enormous sacrifices in pursuit of peace—withdrawals from Sinai, Gaza, and Southern Lebanon—only to be met with more violence. The world must recognize that peace is not achieved through endless concessions, but through the defeat of ideologies that glorify destruction over coexistence.

GLOBAL SOLIDARITY: THE DUTY OF ALL DEMOCRACIES

While Israel stands at the forefront of the battle against terrorism, it is not alone in this struggle. Democracies worldwide must recognize that the threats Israel faces today could reach their own shores tomorrow.

The President of Guatemala affirms his nation's unwavering support: *"Israel has been a true friend to Guatemala, and we will always stand in defense of its sovereignty and security."*

Similarly, the **President of Paraguay** articulates the fundamental principle that unites all democratic nations: *"We stand with Israel not just as a matter of diplomacy, but because we recognize the right of every nation to defend itself against terror."*

This sentiment must extend beyond mere rhetoric. Democracies must actively support one another, both diplomaticallhy and militarily, in the face of growing security threats. They must also work together to combat disinformation, counter radicalization, and push back against international institutions that enable terrorism through moral relativism.

CONCLUSION: THE COST OF INACTION

The world is at a crossroads. Democracies can either recognize the existential nature of the threats they face and take decisive action, or they can hesitate, allowing their adversaries to gain strength.

- **The President of the Czech Republic** reminds us of what is at stake: *"Standing with Israel means standing with democracy, law, and the right of a nation to protect its citizens."*
- **The President of Germany** warns of the moral failure of passivity: *"A world that allows antisemitism to thrive is a world that has learned nothing from history."*
- **Zvy Hazklel** issues a final call to action: *"History will not judge democracies for how they defended themselves—it will judge them for how they hesitated when faced with clear threats."*

There is no room for hesitation. Democracies must unite, stand firm, and take decisive action to secure their future. The lesson of Israel is clear: survival is not guaranteed—it is earned through strength, vigilance, and unwavering commitment to the principles of freedom and justice.

.

THE WAR ON DEMOCRACY: THE DOUBLE STANDARDS THAT THREATEN FREEDOM

INTRODUCTION: WHEN DEMOCRACY BECOMES A WEAPON AGAINST ITSELF

Democracy is often framed as the ultimate form of government, but its survival is not guaranteed. While many fear external threats, the most dangerous challenges often come from within. Societies that stop believing in their own values inevitably lose them.

As zEdward Lindenbaum more known as **Eddyforlife** warns: *"The greatest threat to democracy is not external—it is the decay from within, the loss of belief in its own principles."*

One of the clearest examples of this is how the world treats Israel. The same democracies that claim to uphold freedom and human rights often undermine the only democracy in the Middle East. **Jonathan Metta** exposes this contradiction: *"The international community cannot demand peace from Israel while rewarding terrorism and incitement from its enemies."*

This chapter will examine how the selective application of democratic values—where rights are protected for some but denied to others—has turned democracy into a weapon against itself.

THE ISRAELI CONFLICT: NOT ABOUT LAND, BUT ABOUT EXISTENCE

One of the most enduring myths of the Israeli-Palestinian conflict is that it is about borders. This is a convenient narrative for those who believe that Israel's existence is negotiable. However, as **Einat Wilf** clarifies: *"The greatest myth of the conflict is that it is about land. It is not about borders. It is about the refusal to accept the legitimacy of a Jewish state in any form."*

From the 1947 Partition Plan to the 2000 Camp David Summit and beyond, Israel has repeatedly offered territorial compromises for peace. Yet every offer has been met with rejection or violence. The reason is simple: Palestinian leaders, backed by extremist ideology, do not oppose a **specific** set of borders. They oppose **any** Jewish state.

- In 2005, Israel unilaterally withdrew from Gaza. Instead of peace, Hamas turned the territory into a terrorist base.
- In 2008, Israel offered nearly all of the West Bank for a Palestinian state. The Palestinian leadership refused.
- In 2021, even as Israel sent aid to Gaza, Hamas launched rockets at Israeli civilians.

This is **not** a border dispute. It is an existential struggle where one side refuses to accept the right of the other to exist. The failure of the international community to recognize this reality enables ongoing conflict.

Einat Wilf, a former member of the Israeli Knesset, succinctly captures the essence of the Israeli-Palestinian conflict in her statement: "The greatest myth of the conflict is that it is about land. It is not about borders. It is about the refusal to accept the legitimacy of a Jewish state in any form." This statement cuts to the heart of the matter, highlighting the underlying issue that has plagued peace efforts in the region for decades.

Throughout the history of the conflict, Israel has repeatedly demonstrated its willingness to make territorial compromises in exchange for peace. From the 1947 Partition Plan that proposed the creation of separate Jewish and Arab states, to the 2000 Camp David Summit where Israel offered significant concessions to the Palestinians, Israel has consistently shown a commitment to finding a peaceful resolution to the conflict. However, each time Israel has extended an olive branch, it has been met with rejection or violence from the Palestinian side.

Alan Dershowitz, a prominent American lawyer and author, echoes this sentiment in his view that the conflict is not about land, but rather about the refusal to accept the legitimacy of a Jewish state. Dershowitz argues that the Palestinian leadership's rejection of Israel's right to exist as a Jewish state is the root cause of the ongoing conflict. He points to the fact that Israel has repeatedly offered to negotiate a two-state solution, only to be met with rejection and violence from Palestinian leaders who continue to deny Israel's right to exist.

Similarly, French philosopher Bernard-Henri Levy

emphasizes the importance of recognizing Israel's right to exist as a Jewish state in any peace negotiations. Levy argues that until the Palestinian leadership acknowledges Israel's legitimacy, true peace will remain elusive. He contends that the refusal to accept Israel as a Jewish state is a fundamental obstacle to resolving the conflict and must be addressed in any future peace talks.

In conclusion, the Israeli-Palestinian conflict is not simply a territorial dispute, but a deeper struggle over the legitimacy of a Jewish state in the region. Until the Palestinian leadership acknowledges Israel's right to exist as a Jewish state and engages in genuine negotiations for peace, the cycle of violence and conflict is likely to continue. It is imperative for both sides to recognize each other's legitimacy and work towards a peaceful resolution that respects the rights and aspirations of both Israelis and Palestinians. Only through mutual recognition and compromise can a lasting peace be achieved in the region.

THE DOUBLE STANDARDS THAT UNDERMINE DEMOCRACY

The world applies a unique set of rules to Israel that it applies to no other nation. This is not just hypocrisy—it is a deliberate effort to turn democratic values into weapons against those who uphold them.

1. Moral Expectations on Israel vs. Other Nations

- Israel is condemned for defending itself against terrorism, while authoritarian regimes like China, Russia, and Iran commit atrocities with impunity.
- Hamas deliberately fires rockets from schools and hospitals, yet the world condemns Israel's military responses as "disproportionate."
- When Israel enforces its security, it faces sanctions and boycotts, yet Syria's Assad can massacre his own people without international uproar.

2. Rewarding Terrorism, Punishing Self-Defense

- **Jonathan Metta** warns: *"The international community cannot demand peace from Israel while rewarding terrorism and incitement from its enemies."*
- Palestinian leaders continue receiving international aid, even as they promote hate education and pay salaries to convicted terrorists.
- UN organizations and Western media outlets downplay Hamas's atrocities while amplifying false narratives against Israel.

3. Turning Democracy into a Weapon

- The International Criminal Court (ICC) selectively targets Israel while ignoring war crimes committed by Hamas, Hezbollah, and while ignoring human rights abuses in North Korea, Iran, and Venezuela.

- Universities in the West, once centers of free thought, have become breeding grounds for radical activism that seeks to delegitimize Israel's existence.

Ron Brumer summarizes this phenomenon: *"A right is no longer a right when it becomes a weapon."* The selective use of democratic values against Israel undermines the legitimacy of democracy itself.

**THE WEST'S IDENTITY CR

THE DOUBLE STANDARD: HOW THE WEST FAILS ITSELF BY FAILING ISRAEL

INTRODUCTION: THE DANGEROUS CONSEQUENCES OF MORAL RELATIVISM

In the modern world, antisemitism has evolved. It no longer presents itself solely in the form of racial hatred or explicit discrimination. Instead, it disguises itself as opposition to Zionism, as hostility toward the State of Israel, and as an insistence that Jewish self-determination is uniquely illegitimate.

Pilar Rahola exposes this reality with clarity: *"Antisemitism today disguises itself as anti-Zionism, but its core remains the same—the denial of Jewish self-determination."*

This double standard applied to Israel is not just an attack on one nation—it is a reflection of the broader weakness within Western democracies. When the world selectively applies principles of human rights, international law, and morality to a single democracy while ignoring the crimes of tyrants, it is not only Israel that suffers—it is democracy itself.

As **Luciano Mondino** warns: *"A democracy that applies a double standard to Israel is not just failing Israel—it is failing itself."*

This chapter will examine how the systematic targeting of Israel in international forums, media narratives, and public discourse is not just about Israel—it is a warning sign of the West's broader inability to defend its own values.

PALESTINIAN REJECTIONISM: THE REWARDING OF EXTREMISM

One of the most fundamental obstacles to peace in the Middle East is the persistent refusal of Palestinian leaders to accept the existence of a Jewish state in any borders. This is not a matter of territory—it is a rejection of the very principle of Jewish sovereignty.

Einat Wilf articulates the core problem: *"The world must stop rewarding Palestinian rejectionism. No peace will come as long as their leaders are encouraged to say 'no' without consequences."*

For decades, every Israeli offer for peace—including the 1947 UN Partition Plan, the 2000 Camp David Summit, and the 2008 Olmert proposal—has been met with outright rejection. Yet, instead of holding Palestinian leadership accountable for their refusal to negotiate, the world continues to grant them diplomatic legitimacy, financial aid, and international platforms.

This approach does not promote peace—it incentivizes extremism. By shielding Palestinian leaders from the consequences of their rejectionism, the international community ensures that the conflict will persist. The world must recognize that real peace will only come when saying "no" is no longer without consequences.

THE WEST'S FAILURE TO DEFEND ISRAEL: A SYMPTOM OF A LARGER CRISIS

Western democracies have built their legitimacy on principles of human rights, justice, and equality. Yet, when it comes to Israel, these principles are routinely abandoned.

As **Luciano Mondino** explains: *"The West's failure to defend Israel is a symptom of its broader failure to defend itself from radical ideologies."*

The same forces that demonize Israel—radical Islamism, far-left anti-Zionism, and authoritarian regimes—are also working to undermine Western democracies from within. The tolerance for anti-Israel extremism in universities, media, and political institutions is part of a larger trend in which the West refuses to confront ideological threats head-on.

- **Universities** that claim to uphold free speech silence pro-Israel voices while tolerating outright calls for Israel's destruction.
- **International organizations** condemn Israel relentlessly while turning a blind eye to human rights abuses in China, Iran, or North Korea.
- **Western governments** lecture Israel on "proportionality" in self-defense while failing to prevent terror attacks on their own soil.

This hypocrisy is not just about Israel—it is about the erosion of moral clarity in the West itself.

THE DEMONIZATION OF ISRAEL: A WAR AGAINST DEMOCRACY

Israel is not targeted because it is an aggressor, nor because it violates human rights more than other nations. It is targeted because it is a Jewish state, and because it represents a successful democracy in a region dominated by tyranny.

Pilar Rahola captures this truth: *"Those who demonize Israel are not fighting for human rights; they are fighting to erase the only democracy in the Middle East."*

Those who claim to advocate for justice and peace while singling out Israel with disproportionate criticism are not acting out of moral conviction. They are participating in a campaign to delegitimize the very concept of Jewish self-determination.

The hypocrisy becomes even clearer when we examine the global response to conflicts elsewhere:

- When **Russia invades Ukraine**, the world unites in outrage. But when **Israel is attacked by Hamas**, it is told to "show restraint."

- When **China commits genocide against the Uyghurs**, few international protests are held. But when **Israel defends itself from terrorism**, the streets fill with demonstrations.

This is not about human rights. This is about the normalization of a new form of antisemitism, one that denies Jews the right to their own country while allowing every other people that right.

Here's an expanded and refined version in English, integrating the quotes seamlessly into your book's arguments:

THE ARAB REJECTION AND THE RESPONSIBILITY OF PALESTINIAN LEADERS

One of the most persistent obstacles to peace in the Israeli-Palestinian conflict has been the refusal of Palestinian leadership to accept compromise. For decades, the Palestinian leadership has rejected partition plans, peace proposals, and coexistence initiatives, instead fostering a culture of perpetual grievance and victimhood. Rather than pursuing a path of state-building and economic development, they have invested in perpetuating conflict as a political tool.

As Jonathan Metta aptly points out, *"If we truly care about the Palestinian people, we must stop empowering the corrupt leadership that keeps them in a state of permanent conflict."* This statement highlights the hypocrisy of international actors who claim to advocate for Palestinian rights while continuing to support and fund leadership structures that systematically oppress their own people. The Palestinian Authority has been plagued by corruption and mismanagement, diverting international aid away from infrastructure and social services and into the pockets of political elites or terrorist operations. Meanwhile, Hamas rules Gaza with an iron fist, using its civilian population as human shields while prioritizing the pursuit of Israel's destruction over the well-being of its own people.

If the world truly wishes to see progress for the Palestinian people, the first step must be breaking this cycle of corruption and rejectionism. Continuing to treat Palestinian leaders as legitimate representatives while they divert resources, stoke incitement, and sabotage every opportunity for peace does not serve the interests of the Palestinian people—it only deepens their suffering.

DEMOCRACY AND TERRORISM: A BATTLE ON UNEQUAL TERMS

Modern democracies face an existential paradox: their foundational principles—freedom of speech, rule of law, and respect for human rights—are precisely the tools that extremist groups exploit to undermine them. This challenge is particularly stark in Israel, a democracy that must navigate the difficult balance between maintaining civil liberties and defending itself from relentless threats.

As Miguel Steuerman insightfully warns, *"The true test of democracy is whether it can survive the forces that seek to manipulate its own principles against it."* This is precisely the dilemma that Israel confronts daily. Islamist movements such as Hamas and Hezbollah have mastered the strategy of weaponizing human rights discourse, using legal and media campaigns to delegitimize Israel's self-defense while continuing to pursue terrorism unchecked. Western institutions, often blinded by ideological biases, fail to recognize this manipulation and instead place disproportionate scrutiny on Israel, as if a democracy's right to defend itself must be measured against an impossible moral standard that does not apply to its adversaries.

Moreover, Israel's need for security is not an abstract concern—it is an existential imperative. As Stuwerman rightly emphasizes, *"Security is not a luxury for a democracy under siege—it is a necessity for its survival."* This is particularly evident in the wake of the October 2023 pogrom, when Hamas terrorists carried out one of the most brutal attacks in Israel's history. The reaction of certain international actors, calling for a ceasefire while ignoring the atrocities committed, revealed the deep-seated double standard applied to Israel's right to self-defense.

The expectation that Israel should endure relentless attacks while limiting its response in the name of democratic values is not only unrealistic—it is suicidal. No democracy can survive if it is not allowed to protect itself. The broader lesson for the world is clear: if democracies wish to withstand the threats posed by terrorism and radicalism, they must recognize that security is not an antithesis to democracy but rather its foundation.

CONCLUSION: THE CHOICE BETWEEN MORAL CLARITY AND MORAL COLLAPSE

The double standard against Israel is not just a diplomatic issue—it is a crisis of moral integrity. If Western democracies cannot defend Israel's right to exist and protect itself, how can they expect to defend themselves against similar threats?

- **Einat Wilf** warns against continued appeasement of Palestinian rejectionism: *"No peace will come as long as their leaders are encouraged to say 'no' without consequences."*
- **Pilar Rahola** exposes the real motive behind anti-Zionism: *"Antisemitism today disguises itself as anti-Zionism, but its core remains the same—the denial of Jewish self-determination."*
- **Luciano Mondino** issues a final warning: *"A democracy that applies a double standard to Israel is not just failing Israel—it is failing itself."*

The double standard against Israel is not just a diplomatic issue—it is a crisis of moral integrity. If Western democracies cannot defend Israel's right to exist and protect itself, how can they expect to defend themselves against similar threats?

In recent years, there has been a disturbing trend of double standards being applied to Israel in the international community. While other countries are given the benefit of the doubt when it comes to defending their borders and citizens, Israel is often held to a different standard—one that is unfairly biased against it. This double standard is not just a diplomatic issue, but a moral one as well.

Israeli politician Einat Wilf has warned against the continued appeasement of Palestinian rejectionism. She argues that no peace will come as long as Palestinian leaders are encouraged to say 'no' without consequences. This lack of accountability for Palestinian actions only serves to perpetuate the conflict and undermine Israel's right to defend itself.

Journalist Pilar Rahola has also highlighted the real motive behind anti-Zionism. She argues that antisemitism today disguises itself as anti-Zionism, but at its core, it remains the same—the denial of Jewish self-determination. By targeting Israel specifically, these anti-Zionists are not just attacking a country, but the very existence of the Jewish people.

In light of these warnings, it is clear that the double standard against Israel is not just a problem for Israel itself, but for all Western democracies. If countries like the United States, Canada, and European nations cannot defend Israel's right to exist and protect itself, how can they expect to defend themselves against similar threats? By allowing this double standard to persist, these countries are not only failing Israel, but failing themselves as well.

In conclusion, the double standard against Israel is a crisis of moral integrity that must be addressed by the international community. Western democracies must stand up for Israel's right to exist and protect itself, not just for Israel's sake, but for their own as well. Failure to do so will only embolden those who seek to undermine the values of democracy and freedom that we hold dear. It is time to put an end to the double standard against Israel and uphold the principles of justice and equality for all nations.

The world is at a turning point. It can either recognize that defending Israel is part of defending democracy itself, or it can continue down the path of appeasement and hypocrisy.

History has already shown what happens when democracies refuse to defend themselves against rising threats. The question is whether the West will learn from its past mistakes—or whether it will once again choose hesitation over action, moral relativism over justice, and collapse over courage.

THE WAR ON DEMOCRACY: THE DOUBLE STANDARDS THAT THREATEN FREEDOM

INTRODUCTION: WHEN DEMOCRACY BECOMES A WEAPON AGAINST ITSELF

Democracy is often framed as the ultimate form of

government, but its survival is not guaranteed. While many fear external threats, the most dangerous challenges often come from within. Societies that stop believing in their own values inevitably lose them.

As **Eddyforlife, Edward** Lindenbaun warns: *"The greatest threat to democracy is not external—it is the decay from within, the loss of belief in its own principles."*

One of the clearest examples of this is how the world treats Israel. The same democracies that claim to uphold freedom and human rights often undermine the only democracy in the Middle East. **Jonathan Metta** exposes this contradiction: *"The international community cannot demand peace from Israel while rewarding terrorism and incitement from its enemies."*

This chapter will examine how the selective application of democratic values—where rights are protected for some but denied to others—has turned democracy into a weapon against itself.

THE ISRAELI CONFLICT: NOT ABOUT LAND, BUT ABOUT EXISTENCE

One of the most enduring myths of the Israeli-Palestinian conflict is that it is about borders. This is a convenient narrative for those who believe that Israel's existence is negotiable. However, as **Einat Wilf** clarifies: *"The greatest myth of the conflict is that it is about land. It is not about borders. It is about the refusal to accept the legitimacy of a Jewish state in any form."*

From the 1947 Partition Plan to the 2000 Camp David Summit and beyond, Israel has repeatedly offered territorial compromises for peace. Yet every offer has been met with rejection or violence. The reason is simple: Palestinian leaders, backed by extremist ideology, do not oppose a **specific** set of borders. They oppose **any** Jewish state.

- In 2005, Israel unilaterally withdrew from Gaza. Instead of peace, Hamas turned the territory into a terrorist base.
- In 2008, Israel offered nearly all of the West Bank for a Palestinian state. The Palestinian leadership refused.
- In 2021, even as Israel sent aid to Gaza, Hamas launched rockets at Israeli civilians.

This is **not** a border dispute. It is an existential struggle where one side refuses to accept the right of the other to exist. The failure of the international community to recognize this reality enables ongoing conflict.

THE DOUBLE STANDARDS THAT UNDERMINE DEMOCRACY

The world applies a unique set of rules to Israel that it

applies to no other nation. This is not just hypocrisy—it is a deliberate effort to turn democratic values into weapons against those who uphold them.

1. Moral Expectations on Israel vs. Other Nations

- Israel is condemned for defending itself against terrorism, while authoritarian regimes like China, Russia, and Iran commit atrocities with impunity.

    Hamas deliberately fires rockets from schools and hospitals, yet the world condemns Israel's military responses as "disproportionate."

    When Israel enforces its security, it faces sanctions and boycotts, yet Syria's Assad can massacre his own people without international uproar.

2. Rewarding Terrorism, Punishing Self-Defense

Jonathan Metta warns: *"The international community cannot demand peace from Israel while rewarding terrorism and incitement from its enemies."*

Palestinian leaders continue receiving international aid, even as they promote hate education and pay salaries to convicted terrorists.

- UN organizations and Western media outlets downplay Hamas's atrocities while amplifying false narratives against Israel.

3. Turning Democracy into a Weapon

- The International Criminal Court (ICC) selectively targets Israel while ignoring war crimes committed by Hamas, Hezbollah, and authoritarian states.
- UN resolutions disproportionately focus on Israel while ignoring human rights abuses in North Korea, Iran, and Venezuela.
- Universities in the West, once centers of free thought, have become breeding grounds for radical activism that seeks to delegitimize Israel's existence.

Ron Brumer summarizes this phenomenon: *"A right is no longer a right when it becomes a weapon."* The selective use of democratic values against Israel undermines the legitimacy of democracy to **erode the very institutions that sustain democracy**. This is visible in several key areas:

1. Universities as Incubators of Radical Narratives

- Academic institutions, once centers of **open debate and intellectual inquiry**, are increasingly dominated by **ideological dogma**.
- **Anti-democratic and anti-Israel narratives** have become mainstream in many Western universities, where **freedom of speech is selectively applied**—anti-Israel rhetoric is tolerated, while pro-Israel perspectives are often silenced.
- **Foreign-funded organizations** promote **anti-Western and anti-Zionist** agendas, creating a generation of students **conditioned to view democracy itself as oppressive**.

2. Media Manipulation and the Delegitimization of Democratic States

- Global media outlets frequently adopt **biased language** that distorts conflicts—**terrorists are rebranded as "militants"**, while democracies are accused of **human rights violations for defending themselves**.
- **Selective outrage** amplifies accusations against democratic states like Israel while ignoring atrocities in **authoritarian regimes**.
- Social media platforms allow **radical influencers, state-sponsored disinformation campaigns, and extremist groups** to spread propaganda unchecked, shaping public perception **against democratic self-defense**.

3. The Legal and Diplomatic Assault on Democracy

- **Lawfare**—the strategic use of **legal systems to delegitimize democratic actions**—has become a powerful tool against states that defend themselves.
- **Israel is taken to international courts** over its military operations, while Hamas and Hezbollah's use of human shields, kidnappings, and terrorism **face no real accountability**.
- **Human rights rhetoric is weaponized** to attack democracies while absolving **authoritarian states** of responsibility for their crimes.

Diputado Calixto's warning is clear: *"While self-criticism is a strength of democratic societies, it becomes dangerous when exploited by ideological actors who seek to delegitimize democratic institutions."*

THE COST OF INACTION: WHAT HAPPENS WHEN DEMOCRACIES FAIL TO RESPOND

The refusal to **counteract these ideological attacks** does not just harm Israel—it weakens **all democratic societies**. By allowing radical narratives to dominate public discourse, the **West is undermining its own legitimacy**.

- **Political leaders fear being labeled as oppressive** when they enforce security measures, leading to **paralysis in decision-making**.
- **Security forces are restrained** by **international criticism**, allowing terrorists and extremists **to operate**

freely.
- **Democratic citizens are misled** into believing **that their own governments are the problem**, rather than recognizing the real threats from **radical ideologies and authoritarian actors**.

A WORLD WITHOUT DEMOCRATIC SELF-DEFENSE

If democracies fail to **stand up for themselves**, the consequences will be severe:

- **Terrorism will escalate**, as extremists see that **democracies are unwilling to defend themselves**.
- **Democratic alliances will weaken**, as **countries facing similar threats are discouraged from cooperating**.
- **Authoritarian regimes will become emboldened**, knowing that the international system **only punishes democratic states**.

CONCLUSION: DEFENDING DEMOCRACY REQUIRES MORAL CLARITY AND ACTION

The **battle for democracy is not just fought on the battlefield**—it is fought in classrooms, in the media, and in international institutions.

- **Guillermo Holzman** warns that *"The global battle today is not just military; it is ideological, fought in classrooms, in the media, and in institutions."*
- **Senator Jaime Quintana** emphasizes that *"If democracies do not wake up to the double standards of international organizations, they will find themselves*

isolated in their own defense."
- **Diputado Calisto** insists: *"The survival of democracy depends on its ability to distinguish between legitimate criticism and attempts to dismantle it."*

- *Defending democracy requires both moral clarity and action. It is not enough to simply pay lip service to democratic ideals; we must actively work to uphold them in the face of challenges and threats. This means being vigilant against attempts to undermine democracy, whether they come from within or from external sources.*

-

- *We must also be willing to take a stand for democracy, even when it is difficult or unpopular to do so. This may mean speaking out against injustices, supporting democratic movements in other countries, or holding our own leaders accountable for their actions. It may also mean being willing to make personal sacrifices for the greater good of democracy.*

-

- *Ultimately, defending democracy is a moral imperative. It is not just a political system, but a set of values and principles that are worth fighting for. By maintaining moral clarity and taking decisive action, we can ensure that democracy continues to thrive and flourish for generations to come.*

The Time for Action is Now

Democracies must **fight back against ideological subversion, reject the double standards imposed by international organizations**, and **actively counter disinformation** that seeks to weaken their legitimacy.

- **Universities must be reformed** to ensure **free speech applies to all perspectives, not just radical ideologies.**
- **Media bias must be exposed**, and misinformation **must be challenged with facts.**
- **Legal and diplomatic frameworks must be strengthened** to **protect democracies from lawfare and selective prosecution.**

The **failure to act today** will lead to **the collapse of democratic values tomorrow**. Israel is the test case—but **if it falls, every democracy will be at risk**. The world must decide: **will it defend democracy, or will it surrender to the forces that seek to dismantle it?**

THE IDEOLOGICAL WAR ON DEMOCRACY: ISRAEL AS THE TEST CASE

INTRODUCTION: DEFENDING DEMOCRACY BEYOND BORDERS

Israel's struggle for security is not just about its own survival—it is about **the survival of democratic values in a world increasingly hostile to them**. As **Sharren Haskel** states: *"Israel is not just defending itself—it is defending the values of the free world against those who seek to dismantle them."*

The reluctance of many Western democracies to confront radical threats has emboldened **extremists, authoritarian regimes, and ideological actors** who reject democracy, human rights, and the rule of law. This hesitation has not only weakened democratic alliances but has also contributed to **a dangerous shift in global power dynamics**.

Israel is at the frontlines of this battle, but **it is not alone**. The ideological war against democracy is being fought **in classrooms, in the media, in international institutions, and in public discourse**. As **Guillermo Holzman** warns: *"The global battle today is not just military; it is ideological, fought in classrooms, in the media, and in institutions."*

If **democratic nations fail to counteract these forces**, they will not only lose credibility—they will **lose their ability to defend themselves altogether**.

THE DOUBLE STANDARDS UNDERMINING DEMOCRAC.Y

One of the greatest threats to democracy today is the **selective application of human rights standards**, which disproportionately targets democratic states like Israel while ignoring **the crimes of authoritarian regimes**.

As **Senator Jaime Quintana** warns: *"If democracies do not wake up to the double standards of international organizations, they will find themselves isolated in their own defense."*

Consider the following contradictions:

- **Israel is condemned for military operations aimed at protecting its citizens**, while **terrorist organizations like Hamas and Hezbollah operate with impunity**.
- **International courts and the United Nations disproportionately focus on Israel**, while ignoring China's repression of the Uyghurs, Russia's war crimes, or Iran's brutal suppression of dissent.
- **Western leaders demand Israeli restraint**, but when their own nations face terrorist attacks, they respond with overwhelming force and emergency laws.

This **systematic bias weakens democracies and emboldens their adversaries**. It **isolates** nations like Israel that are at the frontlines of global security threats while signaling to extremist groups that **the world will tolerate their actions**.

Democracies must **stop apologizing for defending themselves**. They must **expose the hypocrisy of international organizations** that apply **one set of rules to Israel and another to the world's worst human rights abusers**.

The double standards undermining democracy are not only unjust, but they also weaken the very foundation of democratic values. When democratic states are held to a higher standard than authoritarian regimes, it sends a dangerous message that human rights are negotiable depending on the political context.

This selective application of human rights standards not only undermines the credibility of international organizations but also erodes the trust in democracy itself. When democratic states are constantly criticized and condemned, while authoritarian regimes are given a free pass, it creates a sense of injustice and hypocrisy among the global community.

Furthermore, these double standards can have real-life consequences for the citizens of democratic states. When Israel is condemned for defending itself against terrorist attacks, it sends a message that self-defense is not a legitimate right. This can embolden terrorist organizations and undermine the security of democratic nations.

Moreover, the focus on democratic states like Israel distracts from the real human rights abuses happening in authoritarian regimes. By disproportionately targeting democratic states, international organizations are failing to hold oppressive regimes accountable for their crimes against humanity.

In order to uphold the principles of democracy and human rights, it is essential to address these double standards and hold all nations accountable for their actions. Democracy cannot thrive in a world where some states are held to a higher standard than others. It is time for international organizations to reevaluate their approach and ensure that human rights standards are applied consistently and fairly to all nations, regardless of their polit[8]ical system. Only then can democracy truly flourish and uphold the values of freedom, equality, and justice for all.

In recent years, there has been a concerning trend of attacks on democratic values in education, media, and policy. This harmful campaign aims to weaken the core principles that uphold our societies, threatening the freedoms and equality we cherish. International organizations, under the guise of promoting human rights and social justice, have played a role in this destructive effort by unfairly targeting democracies while turning a blind eye to authoritarian regimes.

Education has become a battleground in this ideological war, with schools and universities being used to spread radical ideologies that undermine democratic principles. Students are being taught a skewed version of history that paints the West in a negative light and glorifies authoritarian regimes. This not only distorts our understanding of our own history but also hampers the critical thinking skills necessary for a healthy democracy.

The media also plays a significant role in shaping public opinion and policy decisions. Unfortunately, many mainstream media outlets have succumbed to bias, painting democracies in a negative light while downplaying the atrocities committed by authoritarian regimes. This not only distorts the truth but also undermines the credibility of democratic institutions, making it easier for extremist ideologies to take hold.

In the realm of policy, international organizations have been complicit in imposing double standards that unfairly target democracies. While holding free nations to a higher standard, these organizations often ignore the human rights abuses of authoritarian regimes. This not only damages the credibility of these organizations but also emboldens authoritarian regimes to continue their oppressive practices unchecked.

To combat this ideological warfare, democracies must defend their values and principles. We must reject self-doubt and appeasement, standing strong in our right to exist and defend ourselves against those who seek to undermine our freedoms. The future of democracy hinges on our ability to confront and push back against these destructive forces.

The time for action is now. Democracies must unite in defense of their values, pushing back against those who seek to undermine them. Only by standing together can we preserve the freedoms and equality that define democratic societies.

THE WEAPONIZATION OF SELF-CRITICISM

One of democracy's greatest strengths—**the ability to self-reflect and self-correct**—has been weaponized by ideological actors who seek to **delegitimize democratic institutions** from within.

Diputado Calisto makes a critical distinction: *"The survival of democracy depends on its ability to distinguish between legitimate criticism and attempts to dismantle it."*

- **Legitimate criticism allows for debate, policy improvement, and strengthening of institutions.**
- **Subversive propaganda exploits openness to undermine democratic legitimacy, often using**

democracy's own values as weapons against it.

Infiltration of academia by radical ideologies is a concerning phenomenon that has been observed in universities around the world. This process involves the gradual takeover of academic institutions by individuals and groups who promote historical revisionism and anti-democratic narratives. These ideologies often seek to undermine the values of democracy, freedom, and equality that are typically upheld in academic settings.

One of the key ways in which this infiltration occurs is through the manipulation of academic discourse and the dissemination of biased information. Scholars and educators who subscribe to these radical ideologies may use their positions of influence to promote their views and suppress dissenting opinions. This can lead to the distortion of historical facts and the propagation of false narratives that serve to advance a particular political agenda.

The infiltration of academia by radical ideologies can have far-reaching consequences, as it can shape the beliefs and attitudes of future generations of students. When these ideologies become mainstream within academic circles, they can influence public discourse and policy decisions in ways that are detrimental to democratic principles.

Another important aspect of this process is the control of media narratives. Journalists who are sympathetic to radical ideologies may frame security operations as acts of oppression, while portraying terrorist groups as legitimate resistance movements. This biased reporting can shape public opinion and influence the actions of governments and international organizations.

Political paralysis is another consequence of the infiltration of academia by radical ideologies. Governments may hesitate to take action against terrorist groups or other threats to national security, fearing international backlash fueled by activists, legal warfare (lawfare), and media bias. This can lead to a situation where democracies are unable to effectively defend themselves against external threats, putting their citizens at risk.

Legal and institutional subversion is also a key aspect of this process. International courts and human rights organizations may selectively apply legal scrutiny to democracies that act in self-defense, while turning a blind eye to the actions of terrorist groups and authoritarian regimes. This can further isolate democracies and undermine their ability to protect their citizens and uphold the rule of law.

In conclusion, the infiltration of academia by radical ideologies is a dangerous phenomenon that poses a threat to democracy, freedom, and human rights. It is essential for governments, academic institutions, and civil society to be vigilant and proactive in countering this trend, in order to safeguard the values that are essential to a free and open society.

The **failure to distinguish between constructive debate and ideological subversion** leaves democracies vulnerable to their own openness. If free societies do not protect themselves from these corrosive influences, they will not survive.

THE CONSEQUENCES OF LOSING HISTORICAL IDENTITY

Gabriel Silber emphasizes a deeper, often overlooked threat: *"A nation that abandons its historical identity will eventually abandon its moral compass."*

- **When democracies fail to uphold their founding principles, they become vulnerable to ideological subversion.**
- **Without a strong historical identity, citizens lose sight of what they are fighting to protect**, making it easier for radical movements to **redefine national values in ways that weaken democratic institutions.**

Examples of This Trend:

- **The rewriting of history to erase Jewish ties to Israel** has **fueled international campaigns to delegitimize the Jewish state.**
- **The dilution of Western historical narratives** has led to **younger generations rejecting democratic values in favor of authoritarian ideologies.**

- **The abandonment of national traditions and moral clarity** has created a vacuum that **extremist groups and radical activists eagerly fill**.

A society that **forgets where it came from** will **eventually lose its ability to defend itself. Historical identity is not just about heritage—it is about national survival.**

CONCLUSION: DEFENDING DEMOCRACY REQUIRES ACTION, NOT APOLOGIES

The **battle for democracy** is not just fought in wars or elections—it is fought **in ideas, in education, in the media, and in policy decisions**.

- **Sharren Haskel** reminds us: *"Israel is not just defending itself—it is defending the values of the free world against those who seek to dismantle them."*

In today's global landscape, the battle for power and influence is no longer solely fought on the battlefield. As Guillermo Holzman aptly warns, the battleground has shifted to the ideological realm, where ideas and beliefs are weaponized to shape narratives, influence public opinion, and ultimately control the direction of societies. This ideological warfare is being waged in classrooms, in the media, and in institutions, where competing ideologies clash in a struggle for dominance.

Senator Jaime Quintana's warning about the dangers of inaction in the face of this ideological battle is a stark reminder of the stakes involved. Democracies that fail to recognize and respond to the manipulation of international organizations and the spread of double standards risk being isolated and vulnerable in their own defense. The ability to discern between genuine threats and ideological subversion is crucial in safeguarding the principles of democracy and protecting the rights and freedoms of its citizens.

Diputado Calixto emphasizes the importance of distinguishing between legitimate criticism and attempts to undermine democracy. In a healthy democracy, open debate and dissent are essential components that foster growth and progress. However, when criticism is used as a tool to sow division, spread disinformation, or undermine the very foundations of democracy, it becomes a threat that must be addressed and countered.

Gabriel Silber's call to protect historical identity serves as a reminder of the importance of preserving the values and principles that have shaped a nation's identity over time. History provides a roadmap of a nation's journey, highlighting both its triumphs and its failures. By abandoning its historical identity, a nation risks losing its moral compass and straying from the path that has guided it through challenges and crises.

In conclusion, the warnings and insights provided by Guillermo Holzman, Senator Jaime Quintana, Diputado Calixto, and Gabriel Silber underscore the complex and multifaceted nature of the ideological battle being waged in today's world. It is imperative for democracies to be vigilant, proactive, and united in defending their values, principles, and institutions against threats both foreign and domestic. By recognizing the importance of ideological warfare, discerning between genuine debate and subversion, and protecting historical identity, democracies can navigate the challenges ahead and emerge stronger and more resilient in the face of adversity.

What Must Be Done?

What Must Be Done?

In today's world, there is a growing threat of ideological warfare that is permeating through education, media, and policy. This warfare seeks to undermine the foundational values of democratic societies and promote a narrative that is detrimental to the principles of freedom and equality. It is imperative that we expose and counter this ideological warfare in order to protect the very essence of democracy.

One of the key tactics used in this ideological warfare is the imposition of double standards by international organizations. These organizations often target democracies while turning a blind eye to the actions of authoritarian regimes. This selective targeting not only undermines the credibility of these organizations but also poses a threat to the democratic values that they claim to uphold. It is essential that we call out these double standards and hold these organizations accountable for their biased actions.

Another important aspect of defending democracy is preserving historical identity. Our history is what shapes our values and beliefs, and it is crucial that we defend and uphold this identity in order to sustain democratic societies. By rejecting attempts to rewrite history and distort our past, we can ensure that the foundational values of democracy remain intact.

Furthermore, democracies must reject self-doubt and ideological appeasement. It is time to stop apologizing for our right to exist and defend ourselves against those who seek to undermine our values. We must stand firm in our beliefs and not waver in the face of ideological attacks.

In conclusion, it is clear that there are significant challenges facing democratic societies today. However, by exposing and countering ideological warfare, calling out double standards, defending historical identity, and rejecting self-doubt, we can ensure that democracy continues to thrive. It is up to each and every one of us to take a stand and fight for the values that sustain our democratic societies. Only then can we truly secure a future where freedom and equality reign supreme.

clear and concise, avoiding jargon and complex language that may alienate readers.

In recent years, there has been a growing trend of ideological warfare targeting democracies in the realms of education, media, and policy. This insidious campaign seeks to undermine the foundational values that sustain democratic societies, eroding the very fabric of freedom and equality that we hold dear. International organizations, often operating under the guise of promoting human rights and social justice, have been complicit in this effort by imposing double standards that selectively target democracies while turning a blind eye to authoritarian regimes.

One of the key battlegrounds in this ideological war is education. Schools and universities have become breeding grounds for radical ideologies that seek to delegitimize democratic principles and promote a narrative of victimhood and oppression. Students are being indoctrinated with a distorted view of history that demonizes the West and glorifies authoritarian regimes. This not only undermines the historical identity of democratic societies but also erodes the critical thinking skills necessary for a functioning democracy.

The media, too, plays a crucial role in shaping public opinion and influencing policy decisions. Unfortunately, many mainstream media outlets have succumbed to ideological bias, promoting a narrative that vilifies democracies while whitewashing the atrocities committed by authoritarian regimes. This not only distorts the truth but also undermines the credibility of democratic institutions, making it easier for extremist ideologies to take hold.

In the realm of policy, international organizations have been complicit in imposing double standards that unfairly target democracies. While holding free nations to a higher standard of accountability, these organizations turn a blind eye to the human rights abuses and violations of authoritarian regimes. This not only undermines the credibility of these organizations but also emboldens authoritarian regimes to continue their oppressive practices with impunity.

To counter this ideological warfare, democracies must defend their historical identity and foundational values. We must reject self-doubt and ideological appeasement, standing firm in our right to exist and defend ourselves against those who seek to undermine our freedoms. The future of democracy depends on whether free nations have the moral clarity and courage to stand firm against ideological subversion and extremism.

The time for hesitation is over. The time for action is now. Democracies must unite in defense of their values and principles, pushing back against the forces that seek to undermine them. Only by standing together can we preserve the freedoms and equality that define democratic societies.

.

Its depends on its ability to distinguish between legitimate criticism and attempts to dismantle it.' While self-criticism is a strength of democratic societies, it becomes dangerous when exploited by ideological actors who seek to delegitimize democratic institutions. Failing to recognize the difference between constructive debate and subversive propaganda leaves democracies vulnerable to their own openness.

As Gabriel Silber emphasizes, 'A nation that abandons its historical identity will eventually abandon its moral compass.' Democracies that fail to uphold their founding principles become vulnerable to ideological subversion. Without a strong historical identity, citizens lose sight of what they are fighting to protect, making it easier for radical movements to redefine national values in ways that weaken democratic institutions.

Sharren Haskel reinforces, 'Israel is not just defending itself—it is defending the values of the free world against those who seek to dismantle them.' The Israeli struggle is emblematic of the global fight between democracies and extremist ideologies. The West's hesitation to confront radical threats has emboldened those who reject democracy, human rights, and the rule of law.

An optimist future view

THE SURVIVAL OF DEMOCRACIES AGAINST TERRORISM AND IDEOLOGICAL SUBVERSION

Modern democracies face a dual challenge: the threat of terrorism on one hand and ideological subversion from within on the other, both of which seek to undermine their fundamental values. As **Jonathan Metta** points out, *"If we truly care about the Palestinian people, we must stop empowering the corrupt leadership that keeps them in a state of permanent conflict."* This observation highlights a critical issue in the Middle East conflict: Western democracies, in their attempt to support a supposedly just cause, often end up reinforcing power structures that perpetuate violence and oppression. Instead of fostering democratic institutions, they empower leadership that rejects peaceful solutions and keeps its people in a state of perpetual suffering.

This dilemma is not unique to the Palestinian case. Across the democratic world, forces exploit democratic principles to weaken the system from within. As **Miguel Steuerman** warns, *"The true test of democracy is whether it can survive the forces that seek to manipulate its own principles against it."* This is evident in cases where radical movements, under the guise of democratic discourse, aim to erode the very foundations of the system. Freedom of speech, a cornerstone of any democracy, becomes a weapon when it is used to spread disinformation and incite hatred. Steuerman captures this perfectly: *"Free speech is a pillar of democracy, but when it is used to spread lies and incitement, it ceases to be."*

Historically, democracies that have tried to appease terrorism have failed. **Michael Ehrlich** underscores this reality: *"History has shown that democracies that appease terrorism do not survive—they are consumed by it."* The evidence is clear: concessions to extremist groups do not lead to peace but rather embolden these groups to continue their violent agendas. Democracies that hesitate to defend themselves inevitably find their security compromised. As **Mario Schneider** puts it, *"A democracy that is afraid to defend itself is already halfway to surrendering to its enemies."*

The erosion of national identity further weakens democratic resilience. **Gabriel Silber** highlights this risk: *"A nation that abandons its historical identity will eventually abandon its moral compass."* Democracies that fail to uphold their founding principles become vulnerable to ideological subversion. Without a strong historical identity, citizens lose sight of what they are fighting to protect, making it easier for radical movements to redefine national values in ways that undermine democratic institutions.

Security is not a luxury—it is a necessity for the survival of a democracy under siege. As **Miguel Steuerman** states, *"Security is not a luxury for a democracy under siege—it is a necessity for its survival."* If democracies fail to recognize this, they risk succumbing to the very forces that seek to destroy them. The challenge ahead is not merely to defend democracy but to reinforce it against both external and internal threats. Only by doing so can democracies uphold their values and ensure their long-term survival.